THE COMIC ART
OF LAURENCE STERNE

The Comic Art of Laurence Sterne

CONVENTION
AND INNOVATION IN
TRISTRAM SHANDY
AND
A SENTIMENTAL JOURNEY

JOHN M. STEDMOND

University of Toronto Press

TO NONA

Acknowledgments

PORTIONS OF THIS STUDY were published previously in the following journals and are included here with the generous permission of their editors: *Philological Quarterly, Modern Language Quarterly, Studies in English Literature, English Studies.* Excerpts from an article by Walter E. Houghton, "The English Virtuoso in the Seventeenth Century," *Journal of the History of Ideas,* III (1942), are quoted with the permission of the Editor. The work has been supported at various stages by research grants from the Nuffield Foundation, the University of Saskatchewan, and Queen's University. The final draft was completed during tenure of an R. Samuel McLaughlin research fellowship for 1964–65 at Queen's University. This work has been published with the help of a grant from the Humanities Research Council of Canada using funds provided by the Canada Council, and with the assistance of the Publications Fund of the University of Toronto Press. The valuable help of the Editor, staff, and readers of the University of Toronto Press in preparing the manuscript for publication is gratefully acknowledged.

Contents

ACKNOWLEDGMENTS   vii

I   Context and Meaning   3

II   Genre and *Tristram Shandy*   11

III   The Question of Style   30

IV   Tristram as Satirist   48

V   Tristram as Clown   66

VI   The Faces of Yorick:
The *Sermons* and *A Sentimental Journey*   132

VII   Sterne's Comic View   161

APPENDIX:
Plagiarism and Originality   166

INDEX   173

THE COMIC ART
OF LAURENCE STERNE

Context and Meaning

TRISTRAM SHANDY is a provocative as well as an amusing work and has from the first appearance of its first volumes called forth in its readers a variety of reactions.[1] Over the years, discussions of it have touched on most of the topics relevant to prose fiction, though only in comparatively recent times has there been much inclination to take its comedy seriously. But it has frequently proved vexing to critics, especially those intent on finding an inclusive theory to explain the all too diverse manifestations of that species commonly, if loosely, referred to as the novel. *Tristram Shandy* fits uneasily into pigeon-holes.

Sterne has often been praised as an innovator in the art of fiction, particularly by twentieth-century commentators who have recognized the use by modern writers of devices which seem to originate with him. But many of the apparently unconventional aspects of his art are adaptations of older conventions to the relatively new medium of the novel. This fact does not diminish his "originality"—he made available

[1]See, for example, Alan B. Howes's account of the vicissitudes of Sterne's reputation in England from 1760 to 1868 in *Yorick and the Critics* (New Haven, 1958), and for more recent times see Lodwick Hartley's *Laurence Sterne in the Twentieth Century* (Chapel Hill, 1966).

revivified relics of the past and in so doing revealed their continuing usefulness in channelling and shaping works of the imagination. His comic attitude to his material did not allow him to accept these older conventions uncritically, for, in accordance with techniques of comedy, he strove to seem unconventional, to play the clown. Laughter often stems from recognition of incongruities, which in turn depends on a sense of what is congruous or expected, or, in short, conventional. Comic art thus provides a fruitful field for the examination of the function of conventions in the process of artistic communication. A close reading of the "unconventional" writings of Laurence Sterne reveals a good deal both about comic uses of convention and about the nature of comedy.

In its most obvious eighteenth-century context *Tristram Shandy* bears an evident relation to that protean genre the novel which had come into being in its modern form in the half century immediately preceding the publication of Sterne's work. Certainly the readers of its early volumes seemed to think of *Tristram Shandy* as comparable to the books of Fielding and Smollett, and, when "sentimental" attributes developed in later instalments, the name of Richardson was invoked. But difficulties appear as soon as one tries to state clearly the nature of such relationships. For example, *Tristram Shandy* has no apparent "plot" and thus differs markedly in this aspect from *Clarissa* or *Tom Jones*. In fact, it used to be popular to think of Sterne as attempting to burlesque Fielding's methods. More thorough scholarship has shown that Sterne was quite possibly travestying the hack imitators of Fielding who seized upon his digressive narrative methods to capitalize on his popularity and because his techniques seemed deceptively easy to copy.[2] But the digressive method was not invented by Fielding, and Sterne had a good many

[2]See Wayne C. Booth, "The Self-Conscious Narrator in Comic Fiction before *Tristram Shandy*," PMLA, LXVII (1952), 163–85.

other models on which to draw: notably, as he himself made clear, Cervantes, Rabelais, and Burton from previous centuries. But once these other models are mentioned, fresh problems arise concerning the meaning of the term "novel" when applied to *Tristram Shandy*. It can be readily seen, for instance, that Sterne's book has possibly as much in common with the tradition of the periodical essay as with that of the novel.[3]

Obviously, what one gets out of *Tristram Shandy* depends to a large extent on the contexts to which it is related. This is true of any work of literature, but not many offer such an equivocal surface. And, for the modern reader, the whole matter is complicated by the fact that some twentieth-century novelists have learned from Sterne, so that our attitudes to him are inevitably tempered by our awareness of James Joyce and Virginia Woolf and perhaps Thomas Mann and Samuel Beckett.[4] Part of the complexity of *Tristram Shandy*, then, springs from the intricacy of its allusiveness. Readings of it vary according to the particular relationships which the reader chooses to emphasize, including, of course, its connections with Sterne's other writings, such as the *Sermons* and *A Sentimental Journey*, and with what we know of his life and times.

[3]Lionel Stevenson, in "The Second Birth of the English Novel," *UTQ*, XIV (1944–45), 368, calls *Tristram Shandy* "that chimera of a novel which was in truth a reversion to the discursive essays and character-sketches which had paved the way toward the novel half a century before." (Abbreviations of titles of journals cited in footnotes follow the style of the *Annual Bibliography of the Modern Language Association*.)

[4]Sterne's name crops up frequently in discussions of the twentieth-century novel. Frank Kermode, for example, notes a resemblance between Sterne's kind of comedy and Vladimir Nabokov's "tragic farce"; *Puzzles and Epiphanies* (London, 1962), pp. 228–34. For George P. Elliott, the "special quality of the *Alexandria Quartet* (as of *Tristram Shandy*) is accomplished by something considerably more interesting than its overt philosophy: its fictional strategies"; "The Other Side of the Story," in *The World of Lawrence Durrell*, ed. Harry T. Moore (Carbondale, Ill., 1962), p. 92. And Frederick R. Karl calls Henry Green a "direct literary descendant of Sterne"; *The Contemporary English Novel* (New York, 1962), p. 189.

Apologists for comic works often cite their satiric elements, their "thoughtful laughter," just as defenders of satire frequently stress its humorous aspects as a means, usually, of proving that the satirist is not necessarily a harsh misanthropist. As comedy, *Tristram Shandy* might be said to verge on that part of the "satiric spectrum" which has been called "punitive satire" to distinguish it from the kind mainly designed to persuade and which thus verges on polemic rhetoric.[5] Sterne is certainly more concerned with delighting than convincing. However, the comic tradition to which *Tristram Shandy* belongs seems better described as saturnalian rather than satiric.[6] As in saturnalia, Sterne's book is infused with the "holiday" atmosphere of release from normal limitations. Tristram, like the clown or Vice, is "a recognized anarchist who [makes] aberration obvious by carrying release to absurd extremes." He provides "both release for impulses which run counter to decorum and the clarification about limits which comes from going beyond the limit." But in order to signify a return to law and order, the clown king of saturnalian revelry becomes in the end a scapegoat. He, as symbolic representative of the aberrations inherent in society, is judged and condemned. His sceptical attitude makes him a potential danger to those in power. Only in a stable society can he be granted full licence. In times of shifting concepts, he must, like Falstaff, be cast out. The potency of Tristram's clowning is revealed by the recurrent attempts, over the years, to nullify its implications.

A. R. Towers, who calls Tristram a hero *manqué,* "perhaps the first major representative of a type so important in modern fiction,"[7] analyses the three main characters in *Tristram*

[5]See Edward W. Rosenheim Jr., *Swift and the Satirist's Art* (Chicago, 1963), pp. 25–26.

[6]See C. L. Barber, "From Ritual to Comedy: An Examination of Henry IV," *English Stage Comedy* (New York, 1955), pp. 22–51.

[7]"Sterne's Cock and Bull Story," *ELH,* XXIV (1957), 16. In his book *Sterne's Comedy of Moral Sentiments* (Pittsburgh, 1966), p. 117, Arthur

Shandy as representatives of three kinds of sexual comedy. He finds in Tristram the comedy of inadequacy; in Uncle Toby, the comedy of displacement; and in Walter Shandy, the comedy of frustration. These are, of course, conventional comic postures, as Northrop Frye's "anatomy" of characters usually found in ironic fiction makes clear.[8] Tristram is the *eiron*, the man who deprecates himself in order to show up the *alazon*, the impostor who tries to be something more than he is. The *alazon* is very often represented as a learned crank or obsessed philosopher, like Walter, and, in one of his facets, like Toby (and, as well, the reader who is constantly being implicated by Sterne). But Toby is also, to an extent, the *pharmakos* or scapegoat, the typical victim, neither innocent nor guilty, who suffers for the guilt of society. And Tristram, too, is of course a scapegoat, buffeted by the fickle Duchess, fortune.

Unconventionality, which paradoxically depends for its effectiveness on the existence of conventions, is (again para-doxically) one of the "conventions" of Sterne's comedy. He uses the convention of "beginning at the beginning," starting with the birth of the narrator, but parodies this convention by pushing it nine months back to the very time of conception. Traditionally, only epic heroes are traced to pre-natal origins (usually of an exceptional, perhaps miraculous kind, involving the intervention of a god), and Sterne includes a reference to Leda and the swan to underline this aspect of his parodic humour. But here, no "hero" is involved, but rather an anti-hero, and no god-like intervention, but rather the anti-rational, almost mechanical, association of ideas, described by Locke as one of the prime characteristics of the operation of the human mind. Thus we have also in this opening scene the

H. Cash sounds a warning note: "the differences between Sterne's psy-chological ethic and Freud's psychological analysis are, I believe, more instructive than their similarities," and he goes on to list important ways in which Sterne differs from Freud.

[8] *Anatomy of Criticism* (Princeton, 1957), pp. 39–42.

exploitation of another familiar comic technique, the reduction of man to machine. Copulation and clock-winding are on
a par in the Shandy household, a household that Father
Shandy would like to regulate as skilfully as the master clock-
maker, revealed by Newton, regulates the universe. But un-
swanlike Father Shandy is no god, whatever his pretensions,
just as Mother Shandy is no Leda. There is inherent in this
opening scene, as elsewhere in *Tristram Shandy*, criticism of
mechanistic concepts of the universe, but such criticism is at
the same time "conventional," part and parcel of comic traditions going back to remotest antiquity.

The "bawdiness" of this opening scene consists almost
entirely of exploitation of *double entendre*: the reader's possible misconceptions are played upon and taken full advantage
of. And the lack of "communication" between the Shandy
parents even in the most intimate of acts is closely related to
the difficulties of communication between author and reader.
These opening pages seek to sow the seeds of the narrative—
to impregnate the reader, as it were, with a desire to read on,
and to implicate him, from the beginning, not only in the
events being described but in the problems of getting those
events on to paper. Like Mother Shandy, the reader has certain
built-in associations of ideas. He brings to his perusal of the
first page of a work of fiction certain fixed expectations. Sterne
seeks to jar these expectations, partly for humorous effect
(though perhaps this is only a different way of saying that the
effect of humour is to jar us into new awarenesses by making
us see the incongruity of the familiar). He intends his opening
to be as disconcerting to the conventionally minded reader as
Mrs. Shandy's mechanical reaction to familiar stimulus is to
Mr. Shandy. If, of course, the reader is as upset as Mr.
Shandy, it may be that the effect on the fledgling novel, striving to be born, will be as disastrous as that hinted at for the
yet-to-be-born Tristram. Mr. Shandy, like the reader, is jarred
into awareness. For this he blames his wife, just as the reader

may blame Sterne. Mrs. Shandy's stinging comment is, however, made with no realization of its significance (and this is
part of the humour), while Sterne's exploitation of the conventions is nothing if not deliberate.

One implication of the opening scene is that there are
perhaps sounder conventions for the sex-act than the dull
routine exemplified in the Shandy household, though one
must not overlook the irony that the routine is not barren since
it results in Tristram, without whom there would be no book.
Another implication may be that there are sounder ways of
beginning a fictional account of the life of a man than the
ones then in vogue. But again there is the irony that without
the conventions there could be no comic unconventionality.
We have, side by side, a demonstration of the absurdity of
human conventions and the madness of a world in which
conventions are flouted. The patterns which man's reason
imposes on the flux of nature in an attempt to make sense of
human experience are revealed in all their aridity, and yet, at
the same time, the necessity for such patterns is demonstrated
by the comic chaos of a world without apparent order.

But the "comic chaos" is more apparent than real. There
is a shrewdly calculated order in the very nature of the book's
disorder. The talk of birth leads on to talk of midwives, which
in turn leads to Parson Yorick, who is not only responsible for
the licensing of the midwife who attends Mrs. Shandy at the
birth of Tristram but is also a jester, as his name implies. But
he is a jester whose wit has won him nothing but the enmity
of the butts of his jokes and whose death and epitaph are soon,
incongruously, juxtaposed with the talk of midwives and birth.
Thus the jester Sterne reminds himself and his reader of the
realities of his own role, and its inevitable consequences.
Perhaps this is a shrewd bid for the reader's sympathy
—he deliberately associates the jester with the Shakespearean
Fool as well as the Don of Cervantes. But this apparent bit of
sentimentality is one more trap for the conventional reader

who does not appreciate the ironic complexities of the clown figure, the personification of Folly. Yorick is, after all, not the author of the book. Tristram holds the pen. But Yorick serves to introduce the tradition of the jester, to remind the reader of the minor, but highly significant, role the clown can play in tragic drama. And he also amplifies the point which Sterne makes in his dedication to Pitt that the jester lives "in a constant endeavour to fence against the infirmities of ill health, and other evils of life, by mirth. . . ."

In a sense, all art is a manipulation of conventions, for without such recognized patterns there can be no communication. This is why the idea of tradition in art is so significant—the traditional is the conventional; without it, art is dumb, it has no medium. Thus the study of what the artist does with the conventions he inherits—with his tradition—is a study of what he is saying. Convention, in this sense, is the whole matrix of a work of art, its whole context. A study of the many literary contexts of *Tristram Shandy* is one way of coming at the full complexity of its meaning. Sterne deliberately exploits the expectations of his readers, is deliberately unconventional, untraditional, on the surface. Yet, like many comic writers, he uses this means to bring fuller awareness of the lasting elements in tradition. *Tristram Shandy* is both profoundly original and extremely derivative. It challenges analysis and invites comparison.

Genre and Tristram Shandy

A NUMBER OF recent commentaries have been devoted to "placing" *Tristram Shandy* in a tradition, to discovering, that is, what sort of thing it really is. They have veered away, as previously noted, from considering it as, in the main, a critical burlesque of Fielding's comic epic in prose toward seeing it as part of another and older tradition. But there has been no clear-cut agreement about the exact nature of this other tradition. It has been given such various labels as "learned wit," "philosophical rhetoric," and "Menippean satire,"[1] all of which

[1] See D. W. Jefferson, "*Tristram Shandy* and the Tradition of Learned Wit," *Essays in Criticism*, I (1951), 225–48, and "*Tristram Shandy* and its Tradition" in *From Dryden to Johnson*, ed. Boris Ford, vol. IV of the *Pelican Guide to English Literature* (1957), pp. 333–45; John Traugott, *Tristram Shandy's World: Sterne's Philosophical Rhetoric* (Berkeley and Los Angeles, 1954); Northrop Frye, "The Four Forms of Prose Fiction," *Hudson Review*, II (1950), 582–95, and *Anatomy of Criticism* (Princeton, 1957). Another recent relevant discussion is in Wayne C. Booth's *The Rhetoric of Fiction* (Chicago, 1961), pp. 221–40. In the chapter on Sterne in his *The Early Masters of English Fiction* (Lawrence, Kansas, 1956), A. D. McKillop considers "his position in relation to the general enterprise of eighteenth century novelists," taking into account all of the recent studies. In the last chapter of his *The Rise of the Novel* (Berkeley and Los Angeles, 1957), especially pp. 290–94, Ian Watt has some interesting things to say about the close relationship which Sterne's narrative methods bear to the main tradition of the novel, as distinct from older traditions. See also Watt's introduction to the Riverside Edition of *Tristram Shandy* (Boston, 1965). Other recent treatments are those of Henri Fluchère,

obviously have reference to similar kinds of works; but in relating them to *Tristram Shandy* the commentators have tended to stress different aspects of those works.

D. W. Jefferson discusses Rabelais, Burton, Browne, Swift, and the Scriblerians mainly from the point of view of the attitude to their material which, he feels, they share with Sterne—an attitude of mind closely associated with the scholastic mentality and belonging to the pre-Enlightenment world of thought. John Traugott is concerned with still other characteristics of these writers—he investigates their work as communication or persuasion, and, for him, *Tristram Shandy* is "dramatic and comic rhetoric, verging on narrative."[2] Northrop Frye's approach is more comprehensive, since he seeks to divide all prose fiction into four "forms": novel, romance, confession, and anatomy. Like Jefferson, he is interested in the author's attitude to his material; the "anatomy," for instance, is "extroverted" and "intellectual," marked by the creative treatment of exhaustive erudition. He traces this particular form back to the Menippean satire—allegedly the invention of the Greek cynic Menippus (whose works are lost) and carried on by Lucian and Varro. He classifies Petronius and Apuleius as other early practitioners, giving as more recent examples of the genre *Gulliver's Travels*, Voltaire's *Candide, Erewhon, Brave New World*, Peacock's novels, the works of Rabelais, some of Erasmus' writings, and Burton's digressive *Anatomy of Melancholy* (from which he takes the

---

Laurence Sterne: de l'homme à l'œuvre (Paris, 1961), translated and abridged by Barbara Bray as *Laurence Sterne: From Tristram to Yorick* (London, 1965), and William Bowman Piper, *Laurence Sterne* (New York, 1965).

[2]Traugott contends that *Tristram Shandy* is, in essence, "argument"; that it is a rhetorical *tour de force*, by means of which Sterne implicates his readers in the dramatic situations which he sets up. For him, *Tristram Shandy* is rhetoric which has become the subject of rhetoric—an investigation of the ways in which we are swayed by rhetorical appeals—in other words, a probing into human motivation (see *Tristram Shandy's World*, pp. xv–xvi, 15). Sterne, then, like Erasmus, Rabelais, Cervantes, Shakespeare, the *Hudibras* Butler, Pope, and Fielding, is a facetious rhetorician.

generic term "anatomy"). All these writers, Frye claims, attempt to present a vision of the world in one or a series of intellectual patterns; they tend to see evil and folly as diseases of the intellect, rather than as social ills (as the typical "novelist" does); in their books, characterization is generally in terms of humours or ruling passions; people are often stylized as mouthpieces of mental attitudes.

All these approaches do throw light on the nature of *Tristram Shandy*, but they also serve to accentuate some other problems. Many of the characteristics which they distinguish in the "*Tristram Shandy* genre" are rather different from the ones we generally associate with "works of art." For instance, the excessive concern with rhetorical lists, with citations of authorities, with compilations of items of knowledge, although recognizably part of a definite tradition, does not seem very characteristic of anything which one would feel inclined to label "prose fiction." The writer of fiction, we feel, must render his "ideas" in terms of situation and character—in "human" terms, in other words—in De Quincey's literature of "power" rather than his literature of "knowledge." What criteria does one apply to works of this kind? Obviously, orthodox ideas of consecutive narrative and unity are not very appropriate. Is the material really rendered "artistically" in these versions of the "anatomy"?

I

Appreciation of works organized on other than a time-logic structure is difficult for the majority of present-day readers. Much poetry, of course, demands a complex time-transcending response for its full understanding; but even in that medium, perhaps only Pound's *Cantos* among contemporary works have carried this demand to lengths comparable to, say, Rabelais' *Gargantua and Pantagruel*. In the first chapter of his book, Rabelais posits a rat-nibbled manuscript (actually the bark of an elm tree), accidentally found in an ancient monument, which contains the genealogy of Gargantua. "I," says Rabelais, ". . . did translate the book. . . ." Only the last portion of this translation is reprinted, but the impression is given that Rabelais is more of an editor than a romancer. He has obtained his information from ancient documents and is now passing it on, suitably annotated. However, he is not a silent editor. His opinions are just as important as those of the characters he is telling about. Verisimilitude is outraged at every turn. The characters and the author do and say incredible things, usually in the exuberance of following some notion to its farthest extremities, logical or otherwise. Exaggeration is one of the basic techniques involved; yet there is no single distorting glass through which the whole is viewed. Focus and perspective veer and spiral, never permitting a consistent pattern to emerge. The story of Pantagruel follows that of his father Gargantua, but there is no feeling of a family chronicle emerging—there is no thread of plot stringing the bits of narrative together.

Judged by the standards of the epic, or the drama, this is a slipshod performance, but can it be measured by such specifications? Any suggestions of consecutive narrative which Rabelais' works contain are the results of his use of the trappings of romance to embroider and highlight his principal theme—narrow-mindedness and hypocrisy in the conventional thought-patterns of his day. He carries out his main purpose by burlesquing with generous abandon the ideas which he is attacking. The details of popular romance are only a scaffolding and he does not hesitate to dispense with them when his inspiration leads him beyond their confines. Pantagruel recedes soon after the entrance of Panurge.

Rabelais is too conscious of the complexity of life to attempt any gross over-simplifications. He is too wary of fixed metaphysical systems to superimpose a rigid pattern upon his books. One of the main things he is satirizing is the folly of trying to squeeze the infinite variety of life into the narrow confines of scholastic syllogisms. "Never," says he, "trust those men that always peep out at one hole." A work constructed on such principles can hardly achieve much semblance of what has come to be considered artistic form. Wherever Rabelais' vigorous mind ranges, in that direction goes his narrative. The shape of the work is the shape of his surging thought-stream. Only an intellect like his can afford to expose its creations at this early stage; lesser mortals must employ a form with much more definite requirements to shape their ideas and lend them at least the semblance of coherence. Most audiences, too, demand conformity to conventions so that the effort of comprehending is reduced to a minimum. It is not surprising that direct imitations of Rabelais (like direct imitations of Sterne) have sunk from the view of all save the indefatigable research student.

In that other work which influenced Sterne so considerably, Robert Burton's *Anatomy*, the concept "melancholy" provides the stabilizing factor which *Gargantua and Pantagruel* lacks. The constant element in Rabelais' books, his hatred of hypocrisy and artifice, with its attendant contempt for intolerant restrictions, leads to disintegration. But Burton's intellect much prefers to work within an intricate schematic framework of partitions, sections, members, and subsections, all the while demonstrating the immense variety of matter which can be introduced within the confines of such an unmalleable skeleton.

In Burton, as in Rabelais, there is much scholarly learning, with many references to authority and digressive anecdotes seemingly activated by the desire to say all that has been said, and can be said, relative to each point raised. Both introduce themselves prominently into their books. Rabelais appears frequently in prologues and epilogues, and injects editorial comments into the main stream of his discourse whenever the spirit moves him; but he does retreat behind the façade of his characters for the greater part of the time. Burton commences

with a long introduction in which he explains his intentions
and at the same time sketches a revealing self-portrait. Hence-
forward, the reader never escapes from this pervading presence.
One is always aware that this vast flow of knowledge has first
filtered through the mind which was encountered in the prefatory section and which every now and then becomes suddenly self-conscious and rises into view out of the sea of
erudition which it has accumulated. There is no consecutive
narrative, of course; there is no thread of plot to link the parts.
The unifying subject is "melancholy," but it is the wide-
ranging mind of Burton which supplies both the matrix and
the pattern. The whole realm of his experience is examined in
relation to the subject at hand. Like Rabelais, he does not
hesitate to digress, but the digressions do not set the tone of
the *Anatomy* or provide its intellectual framework. As in
Rabelais' works, this is supplied by the mind of the author—
but much more consistently, since one definite topic is used to
provide a focal point.

Works like Erasmus' *Praise of Folly* and Sir Thomas
Browne's *Vulgar Errors* are manifestly of a sort similar to
Burton's. Paradoxically, they attempt to weld a great mass
of disparate material into a homogeneous whole, and seem,
in fact, to derive some of their principal techniques from
the rhetorical mode known as the "paradox."[3] Writers like
Erasmus or Browne, with specific audiences in mind, could
safely assume that their points of view would be recognized.
Burton, as was noted, did make an effort to establish an angle
from which his literary world should be approached. But
bearings must be more precisely indicated when a satiric purpose informs the whole. The development of techniques of
satire in the writings of Swift illustrates this point very well.
In the *Battle of the Books* and a part of *A Tale of a Tub*

---

[3]To the Greek rhetoricians this was a frivolous composition, but by the
time of Erasmus its possibilities as a vehicle for serious speculation were
beginning to be exploited; see James M. Cline, "Hydriotaphia," *University
of California Publications in English*, VIII (1940), 73–100.

allegory serves to indicate the direction of the thrusts, but in the latter work this simple device bursts at the seams as Swift's purpose becomes more complex. Parodies of a number of intellectual attitudes can be detected in *A Tale of a Tub*; even its disordered structure is a parody of Grub Street formlessness. But Swift at no time remains static in his treatment of his material. He dons one mask after another, satirizing by ironic exaggeration the dupes whom he is mimicking. Unless one recognizes his targets, the effect of the satire is lost. Swift's usual method is to create a situation, or series of situations, in which everything is seen from a certain angle of perception, and within the rarefied atmosphere of which the tempo of actions and reactions is considerably increased.[4] In later applications of this method, he makes his satiric position more obvious: using the same device of adopting a position and revealing its weaknesses by skilful exaggeration, he attacks specific, well-defined abuses.

II

In *Tristram Shandy*, Sterne chose to define his position by providing a fully characterized narrator. "I have undertaken, you see," says Tristram, "to write not only my life, but my opinions also; hoping and expecting that your knowledge of my character, and of what kind of a mortal I am, by the one, would give you a better relish for the other . . ." (I, vi, 10–11).[5] Tristram is the prism through which are refracted

4See Ricardo Quintana, "Situational Satire: A Commentary on the Method of Swift," *UTQ*, XVII (1948), 130–36.

5Page references throughout are to the Odyssey Press edition of *Tristram Shandy* (New York, 1940), edited by J. A. Work. Except for a few corrections based on the first collected edition of Sterne's works (published in 1780), this is a verbatim reprint of the first London edition of each of the nine volumes of *Tristram Shandy*, and largely preserves Sterne's idiosyncratic punctuation and spelling. In the variations in length of the dash, however, the Riverside edition of *Tristram Shandy* edited by Ian Watt (Boston, 1965) has been used as a guide, since in this respect it seems closer to the spirit of the first editions of Sterne's volumes.

the images of his father, his mother, his uncle, and the others. His is the mind which is revealed by the digressions, and in turn reveals the point of view from which their seeming irrelevance has meaning. He does not represent rightness, or practicality, or reason; he simply provides a magnetic field in which the array of minutiae can, like iron filings, form themselves into designs.

Like Swift, Sterne places intellectual attitudes in the orbit of one central point of view to bring them into focus. But, in the manner of Rabelais, he also tends to deal with his material somewhat in the style of an editor. He delights in contriving "sources" on which he can comment. For instance, Tristram must explain how he knows about things which happened before he was born. This he does quite explicitly in several places. As early as the third chapter of the first volume he says: "To my uncle Mr. *Toby Shandy* do I stand indebted for the preceding anecdote." In chapter sixteen, he relates details "that my mother declared," and a paragraph or so afterwards he gives as his authority for a statement that it was "as she complained to my uncle *Toby*."

The reader is meant to presume, then, that Tristram is merely retelling anecdotes which he has had from the people concerned. These he has supplemented with whatever documentary evidence he could lay his hands on. For example, almost in a parody of Defoe's concern with establishing verisimilitude, he recounts the pains to which he goes in the interests of accuracy:

Upon looking into my mother's marriage settlement, in order to satisfy myself and the reader in a point necessary to be clear'd up, before we could proceed any further in this history;—I had the good fortune to pop upon the very thing I wanted before I had read a day and a half straight forwards,—it might have taken me up a month. . . .   [I, xiv, 36]

Thereupon he lays the appropriate article before the reader and comments upon it. It appears also that he has carefully searched for further documents which will supplement his story:

My father was so highly pleased with one of these apologetical orations of my uncle *Toby's*, which he had delivered one evening before him and *Yorick*, that he wrote it down before he went to bed.

I have had the good fortune to meet with it amongst my father's papers, with here and there an insertion of his own. . . . I give it the world, word for word, (interlineations and all) as I find it.
[VI, xxxi, 459]

In this case, Walter Shandy becomes the editorial commentator.

Often the document concerned is thrust into the midst of the narrative so that the characters can discuss it among themselves. This happens in the case of Ernulphus' curse, not to mention the sermon on a good conscience, the *Tristrapaedia*, and the extract from Rabelais. With a great show of scholarship, Tristram at times gives the original of the document under discussion; perhaps in a footnote as, for example, the *Mémoire présenté à Messieurs les Docteurs de Sorbonne*; sometimes as the text from which a translation has been made, as in "Slawkenbergius's Tale" and the Curse of Ernulphus. The mock serious use of learned footnotes is a favourite device, and even, at times, an anonymous editor makes his appearance, calling attention to the errors of Tristram:

*The author is here twice mistaken;——for *Lithopaedus* should be wrote thus, *Lithopaedii Senonensis Icon*. The second mistake is, that this *Lithopaedus* is not an author, but a drawing of a petrified child. The account of this, published by *Albosius*, 1580, may be seen at the end of *Cordaeus's* works in *Spachius*. Mr. *Tristram Shandy* has been led into this error, either from seeing *Lithopaedus's* name of late in a catalogue of learned writers in Dr.——, or by mistaking *Lithopaedus* for *Trinecavellius*,——from the too great similitude of the names.   [II, xix, 150]

Again, when the name of Confucius is mentioned, he adds the note: "Mr. *Shandy* is supposed to mean ***** *** ***,

Esq; member for ******,——and not the *Chinese* Legislator"
(V, xxv, 382).

All this is, of course, traditional satire on learning and
ridicule of pedantry. At the same time, it serves to introduce
the assortment of miscellaneous erudition which seems to have
such an attraction for the Burton-like "anatomist." But Sterne
has taken pains to weave these bits and pieces into the fabric
of his narrative, either by having them act as catalysts which
cause revealing reactions in his characters, or by making them
serve as indicators of the texture of Tristram's mind. Sterne
was in the historically favourable position of being able to
use the techniques of the first novelists to amalgamate such
hitherto rather intractable material. Swift had foreshadowed
this development, but Sterne had the examples of Richardson,
Fielding, and Smollett to draw on when he came to make his
mixture of genres.

III

Studies of genre have been organized in a number of different
ways, but perhaps two main trends may be detected: the
historical approach, which investigates the genre as an aspect
of a particular era, and the psychological approach, which
examines it rather as a manifestation of the attitude or point
of view of the artist. Thus the rise of the novel can be seen as
an outgrowth of the industrial revolution and the spread of
literacy among the middle classes, or as just one more link in
the chain of narrative genres through which man has attempted to express his vision of life in terms of story. Historically, *Tristram Shandy* has obvious links with the works of
Rabelais and Burton; psychologically, it also has certain affini-
ties with the modern novel.

Although Freud, among modern psychologists, has been
the inspiration of many literary "streams-of-consciousness,"
Jung has had a greater effect on concepts of artistic unity.
While he can hardly be given credit for originating the idea

of the unity of "mythopoeic" activity in history and art, Jung has certainly popularized the concept of the simultaneity of all history at psychological and intellectual levels, as an alternative to the more orthodox linear perspective. Some such view of history informs the novels of Thomas Mann and James Joyce, just as it underlies Eliot's *Waste Land* and Pound's *Cantos*. Pound's "ideogrammic" method has been described as a means of doing away with plot in the sense of linear sequence of events, of breaking up the "story" into a number of individual scenes which function as poetic images and are freely juxtaposed for maximum intensity. "Plot" thus becomes, not a simple line of action, but a process of rendering the data intelligible.[6]

So described, Pound's method has certain similarities to Sterne's, although the idea of "mythopoeic unity" may seem too grandiose to associate with *Tristram Shandy*. But in the matter of artistic attitudes, Sterne has much in common with the moderns. Even Pound's "logopoeia"—the dance of the intellect among words—is a fair description of some aspects of Sterne's style. He certainly employs words not only for their direct meaning but, taking into account habits of usage, indulges in ironical play with expected concomitants (to paraphrase Pound).

Pound's definition of an image as "that which presents an intellectual and emotional complex in an instant of time" has been wedded by Joseph Frank with the aesthetic concepts of space and time which Lessing propounded in the *Laokoon*.[7] According to this point of view, the modern break-up of the

[6]See Hugh Kenner, *The Poetry of Ezra Pound* (London, 1951), p. 198.

[7]"Spatial Form in Modern Literature," *Sewanee Review*, LIII (Spring, Summer, Autumn, 1945), reprinted in part in *Critiques and Essays on Modern Fiction*, ed. John W. Aldridge (New York, 1952), pp. 43–66. In his book *Time and the Novel* (London, 1952), p. 187, A. A. Mendilow notes that Diderot, who was impressed and influenced by Sterne, furnished Lessing with many of his ideas in his article on "Composition" in the *Encyclopédie*, and that "Lessing himself . . . proclaimed that he would have given ten years of his own life to prolong Sterne's by one."

conventional narrative is an attempt, on the part of the novelist, to "spatialize time." Lessing said that the nature of language made it necessary for writers to present their ideas in some form of narrative sequence, whereas form in the plastic arts was, of necessity, the spatial representation of objects juxtaposed in an instant of time. Modern poets such as Eliot and Pound, and modern novelists such as Proust and Joyce, Frank contends, have attempted to bring spatial form to literature. This preoccupation with the aesthetic concept of spatial form seems linked with the Jungian transformation of the "objective" historical imagination into the "mythical" imagination (what Frank calls the "transmuting" of "the time-world of history into the timeless world of myth").

The modern writer attempting to "spatialize" time must try to construct his works "poetically" so that the reader is forced to comprehend them as wholes, to be aware simultaneously of the entire intellectual and emotional complex which they represent. Logically, these works can never be read; they can only be re-read. Plot is dispensed with so that the schematizing intellect will not be tempted to paraphrase the action rather than grasp the work as an entity. Consciously or not, Sterne seems to have had a similar artistic purpose. The incidents in *Tristram Shandy* follow no orthodox chronological or dramatic sequence;[8] they are really an accumulation of "data" about the Shandy family arranged in a seemingly arbitrary series. Sterne presents each event at the point at which he considers it will be most effective. The book begins with Tristram's conception, but juxtaposed to it are Tristram's own thoughts on the manner in which it happened. The "amours" of Uncle Toby and the Widow Wadman recounted in the concluding volumes belong chronologically to a period five years before

---

[8]In his "The Time Scheme of *Tristram Shandy* and a Source," *PMLA*, LI (1936), 803–20, Theodore Baird has shown that it is possible to "date" most of the events in the book.

Tristram was thought of. Sterne has seized these portions of time and rearranged them in space.

IV

Sterne's interest in time has often been noted by critics. In his book *Time and the Novel*, for instance, A. A. Mendilow uses *Tristram Shandy* as one of his prime exhibits, and it is the formal aspects of Sterne's preoccupation with time which chiefly engage his attention.[9] He contends that the "great aim of Sterne was to give as true a picture as possible of real human beings as they are in themselves."[10] However, as another writer notes, "Sterne's treatment of time is the *reductio ad absurdum* of the philosophical-realist view of time."[11]

In a sense, Sterne's concern with time in *Tristram Shandy* stems from his concern with the creation of Tristram's identity.[12] Two of the main conceptions growing out of Locke's philosophy are the propositions that men know, not reality, but their own experience only, and, concomitantly,

[9]This is true also of the Russian critic Victor Shklovsky. As Kenneth E. Harper points out in "A Russian Critic and *Tristram Shandy*," MP, LII (1954), 92–99, although Sterne's experiments with temporal sequence are the real subject of Shklovsky's study, he is interested in the mechanical details rather than the total effect.

[10]*Time and the Novel*, p. 166. "This meant," he continues, "the shifting of emphasis from the external to the internal event, from the patterned plot artificially conceived and imposed on the characters, to the free evocation of the fluid, ever-changing process of being." Traugott, *Tristram Shandy's World*, p. 39, on the other hand, declares that Tristram "does not become, he *is*, the facetious rhetor. Since there is no becoming in Tristram's being, he has no 'being time'. . . . Rather the consciousness of all moments, all occasions, all experiences enables Tristram to *place* any event in a context of dialectically crossed motives."

[11]Ian Watt, "Realism and the Novel," *Essays in Criticism*, II (1952), 388. "If the novelist . . . takes temporal verisimilitude to its logical conclusion, his novel can never be completed." In *The Rise of the Novel*, pp. 290–94, Watt discusses Sterne's masterly reconciliation of Richardson's "internal" approach and Fielding's "external" approach to realism.

[12]"Time," says Hans Meyerhoff, "is . . . inseparable from the concept of the self"; *Time in Literature* (Berkeley and Los Angeles, 1955), p. 1.

that the "reality" of identity is transferred from the fixed ego or soul to the separate and shifting ideas which make up the content of the consciousness.[13] Hume carried these Lockean concepts to their logical conclusion. For him, it was evident "that the identity, which we attribute to the human mind . . . is not able to run the several different perceptions into one, and make them lose their characters of distinction and difference, which are essential to them."[14] Thus Hume, following Locke, seems to deny personal identity. But Sterne, also in his way very conscious of the implication of Locke's theories,[15] could hardly write the "life and opinions" of a non-existent personality. He does not, any more than the modern stream-of-consciousness writers, blink the flux of experience which provides the raw material of life. But, like the moderns, he must give *some* coherence, *some* significance, to that flux in order to construct a literary portrait.[16] And, of course, in ordering this material in literature, he is also discovering pattern and meaning in life. From a purely technical point of view, Sterne cannot legitimately be called the first stream-of-consciousness

[13]See Ernest Tuveson, "Locke and the 'Dissolution of the Ego'," *MP*, LII (1955), 159–74, and *The Imagination as a Means of Grace* (Berkeley and Los Angeles, 1960), pp. 25–41.

[14]Hume, *A Treatise of Human Nature*, ed. L. A. Selby-Bigge (Oxford, 1889), p. 259. Quoted by Meyerhoff, *Time in Literature*, p. 32.

[15]Sterne's debt to Locke is discussed by Kenneth MacLean in *John Locke and English Literature of the 18th Century* (New Haven, 1936), as well as by Traugott, *Tristram Shandy's World* (but note D. R. Elloway's comments on this aspect of Traugott's book: "Locke's Ideas in *Tristram Shandy*," *Essays in Criticism*, VI [1956], 326–34). See also Arthur H. Cash, "The Lockean Psychology of *Tristram Shandy*," *ELH*, XXII (1955), 125–35, and Ernest Tuveson, "Locke and Sterne," in *Reason and Imagination*, ed. J. A. Mazzeo (New York, 1962), pp. 255–77.

[16]See Meyerhoff, *Time in Literature*, p. 38: ". . . it is commonly believed that the 'stream-of-consciousness' technique in modern fiction shows the total disintegration of the traditional concept of selfhood. This is true in the obvious sense that the notion of the self as a solid, substantial entity has become quite untenable. . . . But the technique is also a subtle and ingenious way of conveying a sense of continuity and unity of the self *despite* the increasing fragmentization of time and experience; for the scattered fragments of free association make 'sense' only if we presuppose that they belong to the same person."

writer, but he was the first writer of prose fiction to tackle the particular problem of the fragmentation of the self which is the concern of so many twentieth-century psychological novels.

Sterne's delicate health did not long let him forget the imminence of death—he was very much aware of the irreversible movement of time. His method of arresting this flow was not, in *Tristram Shandy*, the religious denial of man's mortality, but rather the aesthetic (albeit comic) search for the elements in human experience which are "eternally true." It is interesting to note that it was with the success of *Shandy* that Sterne suddenly seemed to "find himself." From the time that the first volumes of his book took London by storm, he seemed to recognize the role he henceforth had to play. As Shandy-Yorick, he found in life a meaning which it had never held when he was merely Yorick. And in the successive volumes of his work he continued to delve into the possibilities of this identity.[17] Thus *Tristram Shandy* might be said to have grown "organically"—to be in fact an early example of the dynamic organicism often associated with Romanticism.[18]

If, then, Sterne was in a sense creating an identity as he created *Tristram Shandy*, the "organic unity" of the total work would coincide with the unity of that created identity. After a fashion, as has been noted, the same is true of the works of Rabelais and of Burton, and, in a slightly different way, of

[17]By the time he reached volume seven of *Tristram Shandy*, Sterne was secure enough in his role to joke about his previous insecurity: "——My good friend, quoth I——as sure as I am I——and you are you——And who are you? said he——Don't puzzle me; said I [VII, xxxiii, 525]." And in *A Sentimental Journey* he is even more explicit: "There is not a more perplexing affair in life to me, than to set about telling any one who I am— for there is scarce any body I cannot give a better account of than of myself; and I have often wish'd I could do it in a single word—and have an end of it (*Works of Laurence Sterne*, vol. V, ed. Wilbur L. Cross [New York, 1906], p. 285)."

[18]Certainly Sterne's work appealed strongly to Coleridge, and to such leaders of German Romantic thought as Goethe, Lessing, and Tieck; see W. R. R. Pinger, "Laurence Sterne and Goethe," *University of California Publications in Modern Philology*, X (1920–25), 1–65, and A. E. Lussky, *Tieck's Romantic Irony* (Chapel Hill, 1932).

Swift. But Rabelais and Burton were much more certain of their own identity than was Sterne, and Swift very deliberately adopted the masks whose "egos" were to shape his satires. Rabelais and Burton were able to operate within a relatively stable world-picture (though one in process of disintegration), and to draw into their work vast quantities of knowledge about that world. They were able to use this apparently "unliterary" material because they made it part of their own living human experience.

Walter Houghton has called Burton's *Anatomy* the "first document" of the seventeenth-century English virtuoso movement, and "the fullest index . . . to its range of taste."[19] The virtuoso, "the product and fusion of two traditions, of the courtier and the scholar," was characterized by "the pursuit of learning in itself for curiosity, delight, and reputation." Virtuosity was basically a subjective approach to learning—a "literary" approach. That is why the virtuoso with a flair for writing was able to turn his learning into literature. He was not concerned with "facts as they illustrate or reveal a pattern of law or development"; rather, he "delighted" in knowledge, that is, he grasped facts with his imagination rather than with his rationalizing intellect.

The virtuoso, either as the author of "anatomies" or as the type being satirized in pieces such as the *Tale of a Tub* or the Scriblerian *Memoirs*, stands at the centre of one tradition to which *Tristram Shandy* belongs. As Houghton notes, "the virtuoso stops at the very point where the genuine scientist really begins. . . . A new intellectual curiosity, not yet equipped with scientific procedures, was exploring a world still largely unknown, and a universe still largely miraculous."[20] He sees as the common centre of virtuoso activity "the study of things as they are in themselves for the subjective pleasure they can

---

[19]"The English Virtuoso in the Seventeenth Century," *JHI*, III (1942), 64.
[20]*Ibid.*, p. 211.

yield." But by the early eighteenth century the virtuoso was on the decline, partly because of the "growth of attitudes toward learning hostile to virtuosity." Walter Shandy, like Cornelius and Martinus Scriblerus, is a burlesque of the decadent virtuoso, "a philosopher of ultimate causes" who does not deign to support his elaborate hypotheses with experimental proof. But though Tristram also has some of the trappings of virtuosity, Sterne's work does not mark the petering out of a tradition. Tristram is, rather, an example of the virtuoso in transition, still interested in knowledge as "experience" but no longer sure of the context of that knowledge or of the identity of the experiencer. He is the forerunner of such modern virtuosi as James Joyce and Thomas Mann.

It was no longer feasible, by Sterne's time, to take all learning for one's province without attempting to fit that knowledge into precise scientific patterns. It may be that the virtuoso can flourish only in times when the dominant world hypothesis is weakening—times when the individual, sensing the disintegration of current orthodoxy, is cast back upon his own subjective experience in his search for answers. The artist, of course, always achieves cognition in this manner. But the virtuoso artist is able to take less for granted, and thus attempts to bring more kinds of knowledge into the orbit of his design, a design which he himself must supply. The eighteenth- and nineteenth-century writers of prose fiction were, by and large, content to follow the epic and the drama in constructing plot patterns for their works. They exposed their characters to "conflicts," led them into crises, and eventually brought them to the haven of marriage or of death. Underlying such plots was the assumption either that life beyond the grave justifies life on earth, or (as the influence of science spread) that there does exist definite "progress" on this earth which makes worthwhile all the attendant hardships. The typical stress, even when the governing concept was a religious one, was on "accomplishment" within time. The twentieth-century experimental novel, a product of an age in which belief in progress has radically weakened, has been marked by attempts to escape from linear time, usually into some sort of cyclical domain beyond time.

Long before the moderns, Sterne was engaged in an effort similar to theirs. But once he had abandoned "clock-time" in favour of "thought-time," he faced the structural problem of devising a coherent form for the resulting flux. It is really the same problem faced by Proust and Joyce and Mann in our century. Once he had cast off the simple duration plot in an effort to lessen the gap between art and life, it was almost inevitable that he would arrive at what B. H. Lehman has called the greatest *non sequitur* of all—the fact that reality is its own hypothesis.[21] The constant expansion of a hypothesis to fit the facts can only end in a view of nature as perceived by a given mind.

Like the moderns, then, Sterne took as the subject matter of his books the human mind, in an attempt to find coherence in the flux of experience. As an artist, rather than a philosopher or psychologist, he was interested in theory only as it manifested itself in experience. He did not, as did Fielding and Richardson and Defoe, write consecutive narrative. His purpose was, not to tell a story, but to examine the drama inherent in the very act of writing a book—the give and take between author and reader, the eager efforts of the one to overcome the stolid indifference of the other. Thus Sterne was extremely conscious not only of the workings of his own mind during the act of creation but also of the possible actions and reactions in the minds of his readers. The twentieth-century stream-of-consciousness novelist attempts to deal realistically with the areas of experience described by modern psychology. In a sense, Sterne was dealing with mental areas brought to the attention of his age by the psychology of Locke. But to

[21]"Of Time, Personality, and the Author," *University of California Publications in English*, VIII (1941), 233–50.

present a picture of the mind in action was not by any means his primary aim.

Sterne was not, like so many moderns, attempting to fabricate case histories. He put his cards on the table, openly asserting that he was providing data concerning no mind but that of his narrator—though he made some shrewd guesses about the way some of his readers would react to the stimuli with which he provided them. All language, modern linguists are never tired of reminding us, is originally speech. But what, ask the psychologists, comes before speech? Thought? But what is thought? And who is the thinker? Sterne's "modernity" lies in his concern with this very problem. Probably Locke drew his attention to it, and certainly Locke supplied some possible answers with which he could experiment. Since he was an artist, he translated Locke's theories into human terms, into concrete situations; just as in our time Proust translated Bergson, and Joyce translated Freud and Jung. And, again like Proust and Joyce, Sterne's concern was with "time," and with the ceaseless human effort to escape from its tyranny.

The Question of Style

WHEN THE LITERARY CRITIC considers the tradition to which a work belongs in order to determine the underlying conventions which help to shape it, he usually has questions of genre in mind. But there are, of course, other factors which impose conventional order on a work of literature—for example, the patterns of the language in which it is written. This aspect has never been neglected in poetry, since poetic language is so obviously not prosaic. But the "style" of prose works of the imagination is rather more difficult to deal with. A common procedure in stylistic analysis is to detect deviations from the "norm," then to try to relate these to the personality of the author, and finally to throw light on his work as a whole. "Le style" and "l'homme" are still, as a rule, the main factors in the stylistic equation.[1] The critic seeks for signs of individuality, using as his measure, very often, a rather impressionistic

[1]Here, for example, is a fairly recent pronouncement by a well-known authority on English prose style: "It is the voice that we try to hear, the tenor of speaking and writing, the being of the man behind the intellectual meaning, the being that created the object just so and not otherwise. That perhaps is the final endeavor of criticism . . ."; Bonamy Dobrée, "Some Remarks on Prose in England Today," *Sewanee Review*, LXIII (1955), 631–46. A concise account of modern methods of stylistic analysis is given by Stephen Ullman in "Style and Personality," *A Review of English Literature*, VI (1965), 21–31.

concept of what is "normal." The conclusions derived from this more or less intuitive approach to matters of style depend largely on what the critic considers to be "normal" usage in the particular period in which the work under consideration was written.[2]

The prose style of Laurence Sterne offers an interesting case in point. H. D. Traill, writing about Sterne, says:

> To talk of "the style" of Sterne is almost to play one of those tricks with language of which he himself was so fond. For there is hardly any definition of the word which can make it possible to describe him as having any style at all. . . . He was determined to be uniformly eccentric, regularly irregular, and that was all.[3]

Traill's opinion was published shortly after the end of the nineteenth century. Just before that century began, in 1797 to be exact, Thomas Wallace expressed the belief that Sterne's manner "was merely the style of an individual," displaying an eccentricity close to affectation, and therefore little suited to be "generally adopted by English prose writers."[4] These two expressions of opinion reflect, not unfairly, what seems to have been the dominant attitude toward Sterne's "style" throughout the nineteenth century. Sterne's prose style was often admired, but it was admired for its oddity or individuality. Hazlitt called it "the pure essence of English conversational style," but he did not hold it up as a model for written prose.

We are frequently told that ours is the era of the spoken word, that, in fact, our new media of communication will soon quite displace written language—and certainly the temper of critical opinion concerning Sterne's style has altered in this century. Virginia Woolf praises the "jerky disconnected sentences" because they are "as rapid and it would seem as

[2]The use of computers in stylistic analysis seems likely to render obsolete a good many current generalizations.
[3]*English Prose Selections*, ed. Sir Henry Craik (London, 1903), IV, 207–8.
[4]*Transactions of the Royal Irish Academy*, VI (Dublin, 1797), part II, p. 70; quoted by Elizabeth L. Mann, "The Problem of Originality in English Literary Criticism, 1750–1800," PQ, XVIII (1939), 97–118.

little under control as the phrases that fall from the lips of a brilliant talker"; she admires the "very punctuation" because it is "that of speech, not writing, and brings the sounds and associations of the speaking voice in with it"; but then she adds a significant comment: "The order of the ideas, their suddenness and irrelevancy, is more true to life than to literature."[5]

In his book *Modern Prose Style*,[6] Bonamy Dobrée commends Sterne for keeping up "the spoken tradition," despite the trend in the opposite direction so evident in Gibbon, Burke, and Smollett. Dobrée seems to see in Sterne the only great writer of the latter part of the eighteenth century still able to "write naturally as the mind would wish to utter," because, like the moderns, he sought to prevent literature from interposing itself between him and life. *Modern Prose Style* was written more than thirty years ago, when the "stream-of-consciousness" was at its flood. Dobrée was not unaware of the art involved in writing an "artless" style, but he was still able to talk rather glibly of Dr. Johnson doing his best "to model his conversation on his writing," rather than "trying to write as he naturally spoke."

However, if Sterne's style is "conversational," so, in a sense, is that of most other eighteenth-century prose stylists.[7] Addison and Swift, for instance, based their style on that of the cultured gentleman. The eighteenth century was the great age of letter-writing, a form which depends on blurring the stylistic distinction between conversation and written prose.[8] Among the novelists, Fielding adopted the manner of the familiar essayist, Richardson chose the letter as his natural medium,

---

[5]*The Common Reader*, series 2 (London, 1932), p. 79.

[6](Oxford, 1934), pp. 215–16. A revised second edition was published in 1964.

[7]See James Sutherland, "Some Aspects of Eighteenth-Century Prose," in *Essays on the Eighteenth Century Presented to David Nichol Smith* (Oxford, 1945), pp. 94–110.

[8]See Donald Davie, *Purity of Diction in English Verse* (London, 1952), p. 13.

and Sterne carried the trend still further by making his novels into a running conversation between writer and reader. His conversational style, however, is certainly neither Johnsonian nor Addisonian.

I

Robert Burton's description of his own "extemporean style" in the *Anatomy of Melancholy*, composed "out of a confused company of notes, and writ with as small deliberation as I do ordinarily speak," may very appropriately be applied to Sterne's writings. The way in which "borrowings" from writers such as Bacon and Burton melt into *Tristram Shandy* with scarcely a ripple does, in fact, indicate a certain kinship between Sterne's diffuse sentence structure and the "anti-Ciceronian" period so popular in the seventeenth century.[9]

Morris W. Croll distinguishes two main types of anti-Ciceronian style: the "curt" and the "loose," with the aphoristic *style coupé* forming the core of the "baroque" reaction against the over-elaborate Ciceronian periods so common among Renaissance prose stylists.[10] Among the most notable

[9]Sterne did not commence writing his books until he had reached his mid-forties, the writing of sermons having made up a major portion of his previous literary production. Just how much his mature manner was influenced by the years of subjection to the discipline of pulpit oratory is difficult to ascertain. His published sermons, most of which were probably composed prior to 1751, contain unmistakable indications of the later Shandean style (Lansing Hammond's *Laurence Sterne's 'Sermons of Mr. Yorick'* [New Haven, 1948] reveals how much Sterne was influenced by seventeenth-century divines such as Tillotson); but letters written by him in 1739 (the first extant examples of his prose), not long after his ordination as a priest, betray the same tendency toward diffuseness and loose sentence structure, as does his first venture into prose fiction, the allegorical *History of a Good Warm Watch-Coat* which appeared in January, 1759.

[10]"The Baroque Style in Prose," *Studies in English Philology*, ed. Kemp Malone and Martin B. Ruud (Minneapolis, 1929), pp. 427–56. See Croll's various essays on prose style recently collected and edited by J. Max Patrick and others in the volume *Style, Rhetoric and Rhythm* (Princeton, 1966). See also articles by George Williamson in *MP*, XXXIII (1935), and *PQ*, XV (1936), and also his book, *The Senecan Amble* (Chicago, 1951). A recent perceptive discussion is that of Jonas A. Barish in the second chapter of *Ben Jonson and the Language of Prose Comedy*

features of the curt period are the lack of syntactic connections between main clauses and the fact that the idea of the whole period is contained in the first clause; the advance is thus not logical, but lies in a series of new expressions of the concept first stated.[11] The description, early in volume one of *Tristram Shandy*, of Parson Yorick's journey through his parish astride his horse is an excellent example of the curt period:

> Labour stood still as he pass'd,—the bucket hung suspended in the middle of the well,——the spinning-wheel forgot its round,—even chuck-farthing and shuffle-cap themselves stood gaping till he had got out of sight. . . .   [I, x, 19]

But this is only part of a longer, looser construction. More typical of Sterne is the following version of what Croll refers to as the "loose" period:

> But I was begot and born to misfortunes;—for my poor mother, whether it was wind or water;—or a compound of both,—or neither;—or whether it was simply the mere swell of imagination and fancy in her;—or how far a strong wish and desire to have it so, might mislead her judgment;—in short, whether she was deceived or deceiving in this matter, it no way becomes me to decide.
> [I, xv, 41]

Syntactic links are provided, but they connect no lucid and coherent train of logic. The narrator seems intent on giving the impression that he is jotting down his thoughts just as they

---

(Cambridge, Mass., 1960). A rather different approach which, as the author puts it, "does not dispense with Croll's type of analysis but simply looks at the situation in other perspectives," is taken by Walter J. Ong in his article on "Oral Residue in Tudor Prose Style," *PMLA*, LXXX (1965), 145–54.

[11]Croll, "The Baroque Style in Prose," p. 432 (*Style, Rhetoric and Rhythm*, p. 211), gives among others the following examples of the curt period:

" 'Tis not worth the reading, I yield it, I desire thee not to lose time in perusing so vain a subject, I should peradventure be loth myself to read him or thee so writing; 'tis not *operae pretium.*—Burton, *Anatomy of Melancholy*, 'To the Reader.'

"The world that I regard is myself; it is the microcosm of my own frame that I cast mine eye on: for the other, I use it but like my globe, and turn it round sometimes for my recreation.—Browne, *Religio Medici*, II, ii."

come into his mind, together with any parenthetical asides which they suggest. The loose period expresses even better than the *style coupé* "the anti-Ciceronian prejudice against formality of procedure and the rhetoric of the schools." It obtains its characteristic effects by using syntactic links, such as relative pronouns and subordinating conjunctions which are logically strict and binding, to advance the idea; and yet, at the same time, it "relaxes at will the tight construction which they seem to impose."[12]

Tristram's "good-humoured, Shandean style," written, he claims, "one half *full*,—and t'other *fasting*," often seems almost a parody of the baroque period. Here is a passage, for example, in which the loose style is unmistakably caricatured:

I told the Christian reader——I say *Christian*——hoping he is one——and if he is not, I am sorry for it——and only beg he will consider the matter with himself, and not lay the blame entirely upon this book,——

I told him, Sir——for in good truth, when a man is telling a story in the strange way I do mine, he is obliged continually to be going backwards and forwards to keep all tight together in the reader's fancy——which, for my own part, if I did not take heed to do more than at first, there is so much unfixed and equivocal matter starting up, with so many breaks and gaps in it,—and so little service do the stars afford, which, nevertheless, I hang up in some of the darkest passages, knowing that the world is apt to lose its way, with all the lights the sun itself at noon day can give it——and now, you see, I am lost myself!—— [VI, xxxiii, 462]

---

[12]The following long sentence from Sir Thomas Browne is quoted by Croll, "Baroque Style," p. 445 (*Style, Rhetoric and Rhythm*, p. 223), as an illustration of the method: "I could never perceive any rational consequence from those many texts which prohibit the children of Israel to pollute themselves with the temples of the heathens; we being all Christians, and not divided by such detested impieties as might profane our prayers, or the place wherein we make them; or that a resolved conscience may not adore her Creator anywhere, especially in places devoted to his service; where, if their devotions offend him, mine may please him; if theirs profane it, mine may hallow it.—*Religio Medici*, I, 3."

This loose style is the style of Bacon (especially in *The Advancement of Learning*), the later Montaigne, La Mothe le Vayer, the letters of Donne, Pascal's *Pensées*. But it is seldom found in a "pure" state; almost invariably, it is mingled and interwoven with the curt period.

All the qualities of the loosely linked, "trailing" period are here carried to the extreme, with the inevitable result—utter confusion.

The samples of Sterne's style quoted so far from *Tristram Shandy* are statements made by the narrator; in other words, they are selections from the "opinions" rather than the "life" of Tristram. While the "opinions" make up an important segment of the book, they are not the only part in which the anti-Ciceronian style is used. The speeches of Tristram's father, for instance, are often Senecan in form.[13] The following passage is an example of this vein in Mr. Shandy:

> ——The act of killing and destroying a man, continued my father raising his voice—and turning to my uncle *Toby*—you see, is glorious—and the weapons by which we do it are honourable——We march with them upon our shoulders——We strut with them by our sides——We gild them——We carve them——We in-lay them——We enrich them——Nay, if it be but a *scoundril* cannon, we cast an ornament upon the breech of it.   [IX, xxxiii, 645]

In the later sections of *Tristram Shandy*, examples similar to those so far quoted are noticeably less characteristic of the style. There is a trend toward shorter sentences, a greater proportion of dialogue and narrative, a more homogeneous structure. These tendencies culminate in *A Sentimental Journey*, in which the anti-Ciceronian period is almost completely assimilated into the general fabric of the narrative.

The apparent negligence of the anti-Ciceronian period, the casualness of its construction, seems to have resulted, as Croll contends, from a definite philosophic concept on the part of its first masters, such as Bacon and Browne. Like many seventeenth-century thinkers, they were much concerned with the relation between thought and language. Certainly, in

---

[13]This is quite in character, since his is a scholastic mind, and as Bacon observed, "as was said of Seneca, *Verborum minutiis rerum frangit pondera;* so a man may truly say of the schoolmen, *Quaestionum minutiis scientiarum frangunt soliditatem*"; *Philosophical Works*, ed. J. M. Robertson (London, 1905); quoted by George Williamson, *PQ*, XV (1936), 329.

examining their own thought processes, they would become aware of the artificiality of the Ciceronian period as a means of expressing the passage of ideas through the mind. Implicit in their choice of a looser style was the belief that the act of experiencing an idea is part of its truth, and that the words in which it is expressed must retain this ardour of conception if they are to convey any real meaning to another mind. Thus they deliberately sought the moment when the truth was still imagined, when the idea first objectified itself in the mind, when the parts still possessed an independent vigour of their own. As we have noted, Sterne was concerned with the "streams-of-consciousness" of his narrators, Tristram and Yorick.[14] If it is the thinker's mind which the anti-Ciceronian stylists seek to express, this is Sterne's aim also. But previous users of the style were mainly concerned with their own thoughts; Sterne applied their method to the portrayal of the thought-streams of at least semi-fictional characters. Obviously, also, Sterne as humorist was attracted to this style by its eccentricities, its deviations from conventional prose. He uses it for comic effects. This results in more "thought-out deliberateness and coherence" in Sterne's seemingly loose syntactic patterns than in those of his seventeenth-century forerunners.[15] Self-consciously, he manipulates the anti-Ciceronian period, just as he does the various other linguistic devices which form part of his repertoire of literary techniques.

II

Like most eighteenth-century writers of fiction, Sterne learned much from the great exemplars, Rabelais and Cervantes. But

[14]He was not, of course, a "stream-of-consciousness" writer in the modern sense. As Melvin Friedman puts it: "In spite of all this complexity and digression *Tristram Shandy* is an extreme simplification of consciousness revealed in the heat of its feverish activity"; *Stream of Consciousness: A Study in Literary Method* (New Haven, 1955), p. 31.

[15]See Eugene Hnatko, "Studies in the Prose Style of Laurence Sterne" (doctoral dissertation, Syracuse University, 1962).

he alone among the English novelists of the period seems to have caught and fused something of the attitudes toward language of each of these masters. Of course he knew them mainly through translations, but in versions which carried forward into English much of the spirit of the originals.[16]

Certainly most of Rabelais' stylistic traits were faithfully copied by his first translator, Sir Thomas Urquhart. *Gargantua and Pantagruel* is essentially an attempt to synthesize the world of obsolescent scholasticism, superstition, and chivalry with that of Renaissance humanism. In one sense, it is an effort to explore the external limits of a rapidly expanding physical and intellectual world. The prose style ranges from the idiom of taproom chatter to the eloquence of the Ciceronian period. Rabelais takes every possible liberty with prose conventions: variations of word order, parallel lists of nouns or adjectives, repetitions, interruptions, parentheses. The bulk of the work is written in the colloquial manner; the rhythms are those of everyday speech. But the range of Rabelais' vocabulary is immense, and he delights in synonyms. Often he seems to prefer associating words by sound rather than sense, to begin with a scheme of word formation and then proceed almost mechanically.

Sterne's verbatim borrowings from Ozell's Rabelais have often been noted,[17] and they serve to illustrate the similarity between the manners of the two writers in such matters as the manufacture of names and words, lengthy word-catalogues, groupings of parallel words and constructions, ellipses, occasional inversions of word order, and so on. Many of Sterne's

---

[16]Rabelais in the Urquhart-Motteux translation: Books I and II (Urquhart), 1653; Books III, IV, and V (Urquhart-Motteux), 1694. The standard eighteenth-century edition, and the one used by Sterne, was that revised and annotated by John Ozell (published six times from 1737 to 1843). Sterne probably read Cervantes in the translation of Shelton (1612), but Jervas' translation appeared in 1742 and Smollett's (from the French) in 1755.

[17]See, for example, Huntington Brown, *Rabelais in English Literature* (Cambridge, Mass., 1933), *passim.*

devices depend on surprise for their effect: his rapid transitions, apostrophic interruptions, parenthetic digressions, are
all, in a measure, shock tactics. They are designed to keep
the reader alert. (The design becomes obvious in such passages as that in volume one, chapter twenty, in which Sterne,
or rather Tristram, insists on the previous chapter's being
re-read because a tortuous reference to Mrs. Shandy's religious
affiliations has been missed.) He also shares with Rabelais
proof by comparisons, frequent apostrophes and exclamations,
and a fondness for elliptical effects. Often he seems to want to
supplement the communicative powers of the printed words.
A blank page or a blackened one, a row of asterisks, are really
an invitation to the reader to supply his own meaning, using
the context as clues. They are a figurative throwing up of
hands on the part of the author at the intractability of his
stubborn medium, at its unsuitableness for the expression of
the subtle effects at which he aims. He has used all the conventional means: a treatise might be written on his methods of
punctuation, for instance. The dash, in particular, is a favourite; he varies its length to indicate the exact time of the re-
quired pause.[18] But finding all the usual accessories inadequate,
he must bolster them with eccentricities such as pointing
fingers to mark points of emphasis (for italics and exclamation
marks are commonplace and thus inexpressive ways of raising
the pitch of the printed word). Only by tracing the actual
pattern made in the air by Trim's stick can he show why "a
thousand of my father's most subtle syllogisms could not have
said more for celibacy."[19]

   Tristram has much fun at the expense of stock rhetorical

---

[18]"I have a great respect for the Shandean dash: it has a part in the
rhythm of Sterne's periods, which would often avoid anything so abrupt
as a full-stop"; Laurence Sterne, A Sentimental Journey, ed. Herbert Read
(London, 1929), p. xliii.
   [19]IX, iv, 604. The autograph manuscript of the first portion of A
Sentimental Journey, preserved in the British Museum (Egerton Mss.
1610), indicates Sterne's liking for wriggly lines. He commonly marks
the end of a section in that manner.

devices, and in this reflects a fairly common eighteenth-century attitude. Pope's "Scriblerus" comments ironically in the "Art of Sinking in Poetry": "We cannot too earnestly recommend to our Authors the Study of the Abuse of Speech. They ought to lay it down as a Principle, to say nothing in the usual way, but (if possible) in the direct contrary."[20] Viewed rhetorically, Sterne's use of "bastardly digression"[21] might be considered an application of "inventio"—the art of exploring the material to discover all the arguments which may be brought to bear in support of a proposition and in refutation of the opposing arguments. "Rules of Amplification" are to be found in most manuals of rhetoric, and always include digressions: "stepping aside of the matters, which notwithstanding bring light to the subject in hand, especially the Hypothesis to the Thesis."[22] Other recommended ways are by illustrative comparisons or similes, by congeries or "heaping up many sentences signifying all the same thing in substance,"[23] by definitions or descriptions "various in words but one in substance," by producing examples and testimonies out of other authors, and by rhetorical figures.

Sterne's use of many of these devices is evident, especially in Tristram's "opinions" and in the speeches of Mr. Shandy.[24]

[20]*Miscellanies*, ed. Pope and Swift, vol. IV (London, 1727), pp. 43–44. The Scriblerian definition of the "Prurient" style, the principal branch of the "Alamode," is also suggestive of certain aspects of Sterne's works: ". . . a Stile greatly advanc'd and honour'd of late by the practise of Persons of the *first Quality*, and by the encouragement of the Ladies not unsuccessfully introduc'd even into the *Drawing*-Room. Indeed its *incredible Progress* and *Conquests* may be compar'd to those of the great *Sesostris*, and are every where known by the *same Marks*, the Images of the Genital Parts of Men and Women. It consists wholly of Metaphors drawn from two most fruitful Sources or Springs, the very *Bathos* of the human Body, that is to say *** and ************* Hiatus Magnus lachrymabilis. ************* . And *selling of Bargains*, and *double Entendre* . . ."; p. 67.

[21]The phrase is his own; *Tristram Shandy*, VIII, i, 539.

[22]Ralph Johnson, *The Scholars Guide from the Accidence to the University* (London, 1665), p. 9.

[23]*Ibid.* This device, reminiscent of the baroque period, is a favourite of Burton's.

[24]The burlesque of an extract from Obadiah Walker's *Of Education*,

He is fond of proverbial sayings (as are Rabelais and Cervantes), such as: "All is not gain that is got into the purse" (III, xxx, 216), or "Heat is in proportion to the want of true knowledge" (IV, 264). Among rhetorical figures, one of his favourites is the apostrophe. He is constantly interrupting his narrative with such appeals as "Bright Goddess," or "O, Popery!"; or apostrophizing his readers, or his own characters. He delights in paradoxical statements, like "the book is more perfect and complete by wanting the chapter, than having it" (IV, xxv, 313), and he likes similes seasoned with irony: "Could a historiographer drive on his history as a muleteer drives on his mule,—straight forward" (I, xiv, 36).

Mr. Walter Shandy has his favourite metaphors, as do Uncle Toby and Dr. Slop. Tristram often uses metaphorical imagery to enliven an ironic abstraction:

> What a shuttlecock of a fellow would the greatest philosopher that ever existed, be whisk'd into at once, did he read such books, and observe such facts, and think such thoughts, as would eternally be making him change sides!   [III, xxxiv, 221][25]

Aposiopesis is carried to the extent of missing out a chapter (IV, xxiv); nor does even hypallage escape unscathed:

> ——"You can scarce," said he, "combine two ideas together upon it, brother *Toby*, without an hypallage"——What's that? cried my uncle *Toby*.
> The cart before the horse, replied my father——
>   [VIII, xiii, 552]

This definition of Mr. Shandy's comes at the end of a dissertation on love which has featured an alphabetical list of adjectives. Such catalogues (a common feature of Sterne's style) are simply one variety of rhetorical repetition. In the 1593

Especially of Young Gentlemen (6th ed., London, 1699) is a good example. Mr. Shandy demonstrates how Trim, by following the rules of rhetoric, could discourse at length on a white bear though he had in fact never set eyes on one; *Tristram Shandy*, V, xliii, 406–7.

[25]Hnatko finds some three hundred metaphorical relationships in all in *Tristram Shandy*; "Prose Style of Laurence Sterne," p. 17.

edition of his *Garden of Eloquence*, Henry Peacham gives eleven such schemes.

Clearly Sterne was no blind follower of traditional rules.[26] In almost every instance cited he has emphasized the ludicrous aspects of standard rhetorical patterns by carrying them to extremes or otherwise parodying them. His attitude to rhetoric is thus comparable to his attitude to language in general. Words and figures alike are subjected to his quizzical scrutiny before being allowed to pass. Both Sterne and Rabelais, then, use language very self-consciously, like *raconteurs* who are also listeners to their own words. There is, however, in Sterne little sense of the autonomy of the word. His coinages are mainly playful, they are never exploratory thrusts into the unknown. In Rabelais, there is a sense of richness, of the Renaissance urge to encompass all knowledge in its grasp. His use of language is generously expansive; Sterne's is critically selective.

III

Rabelais' style has been described as the orchestration of ideas: an idea is passed through two or more different vocabularies as a musical theme is taken up by different instruments. Modern commentators on Cervantes have stressed what Leo Spitzer calls his "perspectivistic" attitude toward his material.[27] He uses words neither as an expansion of "life," like Rabelais, nor as depositories of "truth," like the mediaevalists. His attitude is most clearly reflected in the instability and variety of the names he gives to his characters, as if he desired to show the different aspects under which they may appear to others.[28]

---

[26]William J. Farrell discusses Sterne's comic use of "the figures, gestures, and *topoi* of traditional rhetoric" in "Nature Versus Art as a Comic Pattern in *Tristram Shandy*," ELH, XXX (1963), 16–35.

[27]"Linguistic Perspectivism in the 'Don Quijote'," in *Linguistics and Literary History* (Princeton, 1948), pp. 41–85.

[28]Before adopting his knightly title, Quixote bore the name Quixada, or it might have been Quesada, or (and, according to Cervantes, more possibly) Quixana. Sancho Panza's wife is sometimes called Juana, then later Mari, and still later Teresa.

In part, of course, this toying with names is a satirical thrust at the pseudo-historicism of the chivalric novels, with their learned references to many sources, which Cervantes was burlesquing. But he was also allowing his critical intelligence to play with mediaeval philological ideas concerning names.

The importance attached to names in the Bible (particularly the names of God, and the change of name subsequent to baptism) led the mediaeval etymologist to trace direct relationships between words vaguely associated because of their homonymic ring. He sought edifying ideal possibilities as evidence of the working of the divine in the world. Cervantes uses the same device to reveal the inherent ambiguity of words when viewed from different perspectives. He coins names and puts into them meanings other than those conceived of by the characters themselves. His treatment of common nouns affords another example of this approach. Characteristically he allows two linguistic standards to clash—standards determined mainly by social status. This is chiefly exemplified in the give and take between Sancho and his master, though there are many other examples. The same linguistic "perspectivism" is revealed in his tolerant attitude toward dialects and jargons, and in his liking for puns.

Sterne shares much of Cervantes' "perspectivism." One of Mr. Shandy's pet theories is concerned with the magic power of names, and Sterne leaves no doubt about the Cervantean parallel:

The Hero of *Cervantes* argued not the point with more seriousness,——nor had he more faith,——or more to say on the powers of Necromancy in dishonouring his deeds,—or on DULCINEA'S name, in shedding lustre upon them, than my father had on those of TRISMEGISTUS or ARCHIMEDES, on the one hand,—or of NYKY and SIMKIN on the other. [I, xix, 50][29]

[29]Examination of the manuscript of *A Sentimental Journey* reveals something of Sterne's own concern with names. He has carefully revised his pseudonym for Smollett from *Smeldungus* to *Smelfungus*, not, however, in order to render it less objectionable, but rather so that *Mundungus*, used in the same chapter, should not seem too repetitious. His name for Yorick's

The linguistic effects are less obvious in *A Sentimental Journey* than in *Tristram Shandy*. There are fewer verbal pyrotechnics, almost no direct traces of Rabelais. But all of Sterne's writings are permeated with a sense of the relative nature of language. Uncle Toby wherever possible takes the military meaning of words, while "mortar" used in a military sense immediately suggests the mixing of medicines to expectant father Shandy (III, xxii, 205). On the other hand, even words such as "love" and "passion" have rather different connotations for naïve Toby than they do for the Widow Wadman or, for that matter, Corporal Trim.

Ambiguities have an endless fascination for Sterne. As a humorist, he makes much use of *double entendre*. He is always conscious of the shades of meaning which may reside even in such innocent words as "nose" or "whiskers," and he derives a great deal of amusement from the stock device of replacing a possibly indelicate term with a row of asterisks, often pausing after the hiatus to offer several interpretations of the gap (cf. II, vi, 100–101). Puns appear frequently in his pages, ranging from the crude efforts of Dr. Slop which so disgust Mr. Shandy (II, xii, 111), through such plays on words as Tristram's meditation that if his nose had not been squashed flat at his birth, "thy affairs had not been so depress'd —(at least by the depression of thy nose)" (III, viii, 166), to Yorick's classic pun which ends *Tristram Shandy*.

Puns and double meanings emphasize the unstable nature of language, its dynamic qualities which are so difficult to control. One can never really be sure of saying what one means. This is the aspect of words that Sterne never forgets. And he does not restrict his awareness of it merely to the conventional forms of communication. He is extremely conscious of the part which gestures and exclamations play in supplementing and refining the meaning that words alone fail to convey. Sometimes a grunt proves more expressive

---

servant he amends from Le Fleur to La Fleur, allowing the exigencies of grammar to triumph over the imponderables of sex.

than a paragraph, but even an exclamation can mean different things to different people, as in the case of Phutatorius' cry of "Zounds!" at the canonical dinner. Uncle Toby whistles half a dozen bars of *Lillabullero* as "the usual channel thro' which his passions got vent . . . when any thing, which he deem'd very absurd, was offer'd" (I, xxi, 69), and various pshaws, pughs, whews, pishes, and hems, are voiced by sundry characters from time to time. Sterne is quite capable of recording a conversation made up almost entirely of exclamations and gestures (V, i, 347).

Posture and gesture, of course, provide a subtle supplementary language, and Sterne, possibly influenced by the drama (he was a great admirer of Garrick), or more probably through his experience in the pulpit, takes great pains to keep his readers aware of the manner in which his characters deliver their speeches. When it comes to the actual reading of the sermon by Trim, Sterne's professional knowledge surges to the fore, and he is most explicit:

> So much for Corporal *Trim*'s body and legs.—He held the sermon loosely,—not carelessly, in his left-hand, raised something above his stomach, and detach'd a little from his breast;——his right-arm falling negligently by his side, as nature and the laws of gravity ordered it,—but with the palm of it open and turned towards his audience, ready to aid the sentiment, in case it stood in need.   [II, xvii, 123]

Expressions are described with scientific precision; even blushes may have various meanings according to their shades (II, v, 97). Sterne's descriptions of his characters' posturings sometimes read like the stage directions in a George Bernard Shaw play, and quite likely he had his eye on the drama as a possible *métier*.[30] "O *Garrick!*" Tristram comments at one point,

---

[30]*Tristram Shandy* was, in fact, dramatized by Leonard MacNally in 1783. But *Tristram Shandy, a sentimental Shandean bagatelle, in two acts,* makes rather dull reading. The amours of Uncle Toby and the Widow Wadman furnish the main action, with Tristram's birth (off-stage) providing an obstetrical sub-plot. The B.B.C. has presented a radio version of the "amours" on the Third Programme.

"what a rich scene of this would thy exquisite powers make! and how gladly would I write such another to avail myself of thy immortality, and secure my own behind it" (IV, vii, 278). On another occasion he makes Garrick's delivery of a soliloquy serve as an illustration of the importance of expression to meaning (III, xii, 180).

But the writer cannot escape the tyranny of words, even though he uses them to describe gestures. Sterne differs from most other eighteenth-century novelists, however, in that his mind is fixed as much on the word as on the idea which he is seeking to express. Language is not merely raw material which he, as artist, must shape; it is also a problem to be analyzed and discussed. It is a character in its own right, both subject and object, telling the story and being told about.

Sterne adapts the styles of Rabelais and Cervantes to his own purposes. Rabelaisian effects occur mainly in passages attributed to Tristram, and help to individualize him as a character—distinguishing him, for instance, from Yorick, the narrator of *A Sentimental Journey*. Thus it is mainly the externals of Rabelais' style which find their way into *Tristram Shandy*. The influence of Cervantes, on the other hand, goes somewhat deeper. Sterne's whole sceptical and critical attitude toward language is, in fact, very much in accord with the temper of *Don Quixote*. Even his toying with Rabelaisian "galimatias" is infected by it. He never allows himself to be carried away by a burst of Gargantuan exuberance, but always steps aside in time to join in the general laughter at such ridiculous caperings. Thus Sterne manages a sort of amalgam of the styles of Cervantes and Rabelais, producing a style of language which has echoes of both, but which is different from either.

Sterne seems to share the twentieth-century distrust of artifice, though, of course, he is also part of the eighteenth-century movement away from the rigid conventions of society back to the unspoiled art of the noble savage. But language is itself rigidly conventional—it has to be in order to function effectively in a society. In attempting to keep himself and his reader aware of the compromises necessary in all forms of verbal art, Sterne inevitably subjected his artistic medium, language, to critical scrutiny. Paradoxically, in so doing, he was, in fact, adapting well-established conventions of the previous century.

Tristram as Satirist

THE EIGHTEENTH CENTURY is often summed up as the age in which the appeal to reason was gradually superseded by the appeal to the heart; *cogito ergo sum* was replaced by *je sens donc je suis*.[1] This is a convenient formula, and much of the literature of the time fits into it rather neatly. Early eighteenth-century satire, such as that of Swift and Pope, launched attacks on the misuse of reason and on those who allowed themselves to be dominated by their passions. As the century advanced, such satire softened into sentimental comedy—Congreve was replaced by Goldsmith. The writings of Sterne, coming as they do in the third quarter of the century, seem to support this thesis admirably. "Dear Sensibility" dominates *A Sentimental Journey*, and the tone of *Tristram Shandy* is manifestly different from that of *A Tale of a Tub*—it is far less biting, much more good-humoured. If, however, *Tristram Shandy* is viewed simply as one more piece of evidence demonstrating the change from scintillating wit to whimsical buffoonery, then the conclusion may well follow that Sterne's clowning is finally of little consequence, that it contains no "positive implications," that it is, if anything, negative.[2] On

---

[1] See Basil Willey, *The Eighteenth Century Background* (London, 1940), p. 108.

[2] See, for example, Edward N. Hooker, "Humour in the Age of Pope,"

the other hand, Sterne obviously introduces many of the same satiric butts as do Swift and Pope, even though his treatment of them differs from theirs.

I

A comparison of *Tristram Shandy* with, for example, the *Memoirs of Martinus Scriblerus* reveals the similarity in objects chosen for attack by Sterne and the Scriblerians.[3] Most apparent, perhaps, is the comic virtuoso, the "philosopher of ultimate causes," of which Cornelius and Martinus Scriblerus and Walter Shandy are variations, but there are a number of other targets. Theories of pre-natal influences, for instance, are satirized in the opening chapters of the *Memoirs*, as they are at the beginning of *Shandy*, though the "prodigies" which attend Tristram's birth are of a much more pedestrian kind than those which Martinus shares with the heroes of antiquity. Walter Shandy, however, in his *Tristrapaedia*, unquestionably matches Cornelius in his concern with his son's education, and manages, like Cornelius, to take a number of potshots at conventional notions. He considers

> ——FIVE years with a bib under his chin;
>   Four years in travelling from Christ-cross-
> row to *Malachi*;
>   A year and a half in learning to write his
> own name;
>   Seven long years and more τύπτω-ing it, at
> Greek and Latin;
>   Four years at his *probations* and his negations. . . .
> [V, xlii, 403]

HLQ, XI (1947–48), 381: ". . . the Shandean extravagancies are purely good-natured and harmless. They conceal no positive implications." In his introduction to the Odyssey Press edition of *Tristram Shandy*, p. lxv, James A. Work said that Sterne "toys with his satire in a kindly, almost affectionate manner, and makes it less a stricture on anyhting external to himself than an unconscious revelation of the triviality of his own mind."

[3]The *Memoirs*, "Written in Collaboration by the Members of the Scriblerus Club: John Arbuthnot, Alexander Pope, Jonathan Swift, John Gay, Thomas Parnell, and Robert Harley, Earl of Oxford," first appeared

only to conclude that in such a system the child may well spend his life acquiring knowledge and then be too old to use it. So, characteristically, he hits upon "a North west passage to the intellectual world"—namely, auxiliary verbs. When it comes to the question of choosing a governor for young Tristram, the whole catalogue of attributes for such a person which Mr. Shandy has culled from his authorities is nullified by the simple queries of Yorick: "And why not humble, and moderate, and gentle tempered, and good?" and Uncle Toby: "And why not free, and generous, and bountiful, and brave?" (VI, v, 415).

Unlike Cornelius, Walter does not ponder the nutrition of his son; in fact, food plays a very small part in Sterne's writings, though in his letter to his brother Toby instructing him regarding "the nature of women, and of love-making to them," Walter does mention regulation of diet as a cure for passion (VIII, xxxiv, 592). Cornelius Scriblerus connects national temperament with diet, whereas Tristram prefers to play with the more common theory that climate determines the character of a nation:

. . . that this strange irregularity in our climate, producing so strange an irregularity in our characters,——doth thereby, in some sort, make us amends, by giving us somewhat to make us merry with when the weather will not suffer us to go out of doors,—that observation is my own;—and was struck out by me this very rainy day, *March 26, 1759*, and betwixt the hours of nine and ten in the morning. [I, xxi, 64]

With mock seriousness, Tristram bows ironically to his "fellow-labourers and associates in this great harvest of our learning," thus combining burlesque of theory and method. Again, in the "Author's Preface," the whole matter of the relation between climate and intelligence is illustrated by some barbed examples (III, 196–97).

---

in April, 1741 (long after most of it was composed) in the prose works of Pope. See the fully annotated edition (New Haven, 1950) edited by Charles Kerby-Miller.

A chapter in the Scriblerian *Memoirs* is devoted to fun at the expense of abuses in "Rhetorick, Logick, and Metaphysicks," and Sterne, in his turn (in addition to the play with rhetoric previously noted), includes thrusts at formal logic, scholastic pettifogging, and the decline of oratory. "The gift of ratiocination and making syllogisms," says Tristram, "I mean in man,—for in superior classes of beings, such as angels and spirits,—'tis all done, may it please your worships, as they tell me, by INTUITION;—and beings inferior, as your worships all know,——syllogize by their nose . . ." and then Sterne proceeds to burlesque the *medius terminus* by having Mr. Shandy assume (quite wrongly, of course) that Uncle Toby is applying it to the discussion at hand (III, xl, 237). Formal logic recommended the use of the ten predicaments of Aristotle as the correct procedure in defining. The "new philosophers" advanced the distinction between primary and secondary qualities which Locke expounded at length, and Tristram follows him in his account of the three-fold cause of obscurity and confusion in the mind of man: "Dull organs, dear Sir, in the first place. Secondly, slight and transient impressions made by objects when the said organs are not dull. And thirdly, a memory like unto a sieve, not able to retain what it has received" (II, ii, 86). And he illustrates his meaning by means of Dolly the chambermaid and a stick of red sealing-wax. His pointed references to the "unsteady uses of words, which have perplexed the clearest and most exalted understandings," leave no doubt that he is on the side of the angels against the schoolmen. The nasal dispute in "Slawkenbergius's Tale" is also attributed specifically to the scholastic mentality for it led inevitably to "a new dispute, which they pursued a great way upon the extent and limitation of the moral and natural attributes of God—That controversy led them naturally into *Thomas Aquinas*, and *Thomas Aquinas* to the devil" (IV, 264).

In chapter twelve of the *Memoirs*, the Scriblerians have Martinus attempt to find out the seat of the soul, and, in the

ensuing satire, align themselves with the reaction against
the theories of Descartes. Walter Shandy is convinced by
Uncle Toby's account of a Walloon officer who had one part
of his brain shot away that Descartes was wrong in fixing the
soul on top of the pineal gland. Nor did he like "that certain,
very thin, subtle, and very fragrant juice" which Coglionissimo
Borri, the great Milanese physician, affirmed as the principal
seat of the reasonable soul. For "the very idea of so noble, so
refined, so immaterial, and so exalted a being as the *Anima*, or
even the *Animus*, taking up her residence, and sitting dab-
bling, like a tadpole, all day long, both summer and winter, in
a puddle . . . shocked his imagination." So he agreed with
the best of the philosophers that the soul was probably "somewhere about the medulla oblongata," and proceeded to make
this the cornerstone of his obstetric theory that children should
be delivered feet first, or, better still, by Caesarean section, so
as to preserve "this delicate and fine-spun web from the
havock which was generally made in it by the violent com-
pression and crush which the head was made to undergo by
the nonsensical method of bringing us into the world by that
foremost" (II, xix, 147 ff.).

The fifteenth chapter of the Scriblerian *Memoirs* is entitled
"Of the strange, and never to be parallel'd Process at Law
upon the Marriage of Scriblerus, and the Pleadings of the
Advocates." A legal quibble is a decisive factor in Tristram's
life, dooming him to be born in the country and hence to
have his nose squeezed flat by the male midwife, Dr. Slop.
Tristram gives the offending passage from his mother's marriage settlement in its full legal complexity, and then sums
it up in a sentence: "My mother was to lay in (if she chose
it) in *London*" (I, xv, 40). Ecclesiastical courts are castigated
in "Slawkenbergius's Tale," and also at the canonical dinner
at which Didius, Phutatorius, and company hold forth on
the casuistical aspects of Tristram's bumbled christening:

——now, quoth *Didius*, rising up, and laying his right-hand
with his fingers spread upon his breast—had such a blunder about

a christian-name happened before the reformation—(It happened
the day before yesterday, quoth my uncle *Toby* to himself) and
when baptism was administer'd in *Latin*——('Twas all in *English*,
said my uncle). . . .   [IV, xxix, 326]

Even a superficial comparison of the *Memoirs* with *Tristram
Shandy*, then, brings to light a certain similarity in the objects
selected for satiric treatment in each. But there the similarity
ends. Sterne has dramatized these materials much more effectively; he has rooted the foibles in vivid, coherent characters.[4]
Scriblerus, like *A Tale of a Tub* and the *Dunciad*, is an attack
on abuses in learning. It is part of the perennial war between
wits and "dunces," between humanist and pedant, a war
which became particularly vehement in the late seventeenth
and early eighteenth centuries in England, because of the
general shift in the structure of society resulting from the rise
of the middle classes.

This is another relevant context to which *Tristram Shandy*
can be related. Walter, Toby, Tristram, all are manifestations
of the dunce. Sterne, like Swift and Pope, was keenly interested in preserving the rule of "wit" by pricking the preten-
tious windbags of pedantry whose hold over the great public
was obviously growing. However, writing later in the century,
and in York rather than London, his view of the situation
was somewhat different from theirs. He could no longer feel
that direct, though devious, attacks on the dunces themselves
could unseat them and loosen their grasp on the leading reins

---

[4]In a sense, as John Traugott, *Tristram Shandy's World*, p. xiii, has
shown, Sterne's characters are *exempla*, symbolizing conflicting attitudes.
Cornelius and Martinus Scriblerus, are, however, nothing but *exempla*;
they never really come to life. If they had, the satire would presumably
have lost some of its effect, since then the reader might have tended to
sympathize with them, rather than concentrating on the vices for which
they stand.

In his unpublished doctoral dissertation, "Sterne's Satire on Mechanism:
A Study of *Tristram Shandy*" (University of Toronto, 1951), Wilfred
Watson has demonstrated brilliantly how *Tristram Shandy* can be read
as a satirical account of the interaction of Cartesian science (Walter) and
Newtonian natural philosophy (Toby) which results in Tristram's materi-
alistic and naturalistic temper.

they had attached to the public. He realized, as did Swift by the time he wrote *Gulliver*, that satire must now be aimed at the public itself, that the satirist could only weaken the influence of Grub Street by making the public more alert. The appeal, then, in *Tristram Shandy*, as in *Gulliver's Travels*, is not to the discriminating few, but to the undiscriminating many, in an attempt to make them more discriminating.[5] Sterne's approach is much more diffident, much more tentative than Swift's or Pope's, and this is in part accounted for by differences in personality and circumstances. But it also reflects the growing scepticism of the age—the breakdown of the common-sense solutions offered by Locke and the rationalists.[6]

II

Inasmuch as Tristram may be considered as *rhetor*, the whole book consists of his "oration." But Tristram's is, of course, ironic rhetoric, the rhetoric of a "fool." And it carries some interesting implications about Sterne's conception of the nature of his audience. Like Swift in the *Modest Proposal*, he shocks the more squeamish members by reflecting much too accurately their own underlying preconceptions. One kind of empty verbalism against which both Swift and Pope inveighed was the fulsome praise of the prospective patron. Significantly, Sterne's dedication of his first volume to Pitt is not fulsome. But it does not take him long to turn his attention to the usual kind of dedication, and he has his innings at the expense of the writer who will sell his dedication to

[5] Presumably, both Sterne and Swift, in view of the reactions of even the discriminating reader, rather over-estimated the ability of the great public to read between the lines.

[6] In philosophy, the thought of Hume parallels in many ways the implications of *Tristram Shandy*. Traugott, *Tristram Shandy's World*, p. 148, notes: ". . . the Shandean world of vague accidents, of jumbled time, knowledge, and motives, asks essentially the same question as Hume's philosophy: are we not living in a world where cause and effect are really a history of our mind? Is our world of ordered relations merely our fantasy?"

the highest bidder and of the patron who will accept such an offer (I, ix, 15 ff). Sterne was, of course, seeking a patron of a different kind—the reading public at large. He implicitly dedicates his book to them by titillating their tastes, while at the same time managing to satirize the human foibles involved in those tastes. Thus, though dedicating his book to the "Lord Public," he attempts to unseat that Lord from some of his "Hobby-Horses," or at least to make him more aware of his "ruling passions."

"With an ass," Tristram says in his account of his travels, "I can commune forever." Not so with jackdaws or apes, for they speak and act by rote. But with an ass, "surely never is my imagination so busy as in framing his responses from the etchings of his countenance—and where those carry me not deep enough—in flying from my own heart into his, and seeing what is natural for an ass to think—as well as a man, upon the occasion" (VII, xxxii, 523). The reader whose responses Tristram can gauge as accurately as he can those of an ass is one who will laugh at certain words in the bedchamber, but abuse them in the parlour. For his sake, Tristram must seek devices whereby he can "satisfy *that ear* which the reader chuses to *lend* me," while not dissatisfying "the other which he keeps to himself" (VII, xx, 503). Thus, for instance, the off-colour anecdote about the Abbess of Andoüillets (which follows immediately after the words just quoted) is rendered less objectionable for the conventional reader by being linked with conventional attack on popery—a popery, incidentally, which is also conventionally linked with pedantic quibbles about matters of doctrinal interpretation.[7] In the sentimental passages in his books, as has often been noted, Sterne pulls up short and thus reveals his consciousness of what is involved. In the same way, in the smutty passages, and in the anti-papist

[7]One remembers, of course, that the Church of England clergy were shown to be just as pedantic at the canonical dinner—and just as mixed in their reactions to the strange collision of Phutatorius and the hot chestnut.

pieces, he is self-consciously adopting conventional attitudes. He is ironically aware of what he is doing.

The crass wrongness of public opinion (including the opinion of those arbiters of public taste, the critics) is a matter often commented on in *Tristram Shandy*. Sterne chose a motto from Epictetus to prefix to volume one: "It is not actions, but opinions concerning actions, which disturb men." The anecdote about Parson Yorick and his horse provides, very early in the first volume, an admirable illustration of the malicious nature of gossip. As long as it was to the parson's credit that he had decided to ride an old broken-winded horse rather than continually be replacing beasts worn out by parishioners who borrowed them for the purpose of fetching a midwife who lived some distance away, gossip was silent. But as soon as he offered to buy a licence for a local midwife, tongues began to wag and discreditable motives were supplied. Obviously Yorick "had a returning fit of pride" and "was going to be well mounted once again." Such being the case, in buying the licence he was merely avoiding the otherwise inevitable and much more expensive wear and tear on his new horse. "What were his views in this," Tristram comments, "and in every other action of his life,—or rather what were the opinions which floated in the brains of other people concerning it, was a thought which too much floated in his own, and too often broke in upon his rest, when he should have been sound asleep" (I, x, 22–3).

Tristram, like Yorick, is obviously an enemy of the affectation of gravity as "a cloak for ignorance or for folly," but he seeks to escape the trouble into which Yorick's plain speaking gets him by assuming the tone of defensive irony which permeates the book. From Yorick's example he has learned early the fate of jesters at the hands of knaves and fools whom they deride. Thus he is constantly on his guard, and takes steps to blunt the vengeful blows of his victims as much as possible. This is an important aspect of his self-consciousness: it is, in part, an "other-directed" self-consciousness. He is constantly entering caveats in the breast of his fair reader—a fair reader who, incidentally, often takes the form of the unfair critic in the later volumes. In volumes one and two, though, we get a pretty clear impression of the reading public as Sterne visualized it, with its "vicious taste" for "reading straight forwards, more in quest of adventures" than of "deep erudition and knowledge." Actually, of course, Sterne does little to satisfy "this self-same vile pruriency for fresh adventures"; he specializes, rather, in "the gross and more carnal parts of a composition" to gain the interest of his readers sufficiently to make them vulnerable to his "subtle hints and sly communications" (I, xx, 57).[8]

III

In observing the reactions of the critics to his first volumes, Sterne undoubtedly became more conscious of the difficulties involved in communication. He opens volume three with Dr. Slop's reading of Ernulphus' curse—a prime example of words separated from thought. The curse is "mere rhetoric," and the whole business of noses, which figures so prominently in these volumes, is in one sense an extended commentary on that instability of language of which Locke had made so much. To some extent, like the scientists, Locke had held out for efforts

[8]A description of the public of Sterne's day which coincides with some aspects of the one implied in Tristram Shandy is to be found in John Brown's An Estimate of the Manners and Principles of the Times (5th ed., London, 1757). Note, for example, the following:

"A strong Characteristic, this, of the Manners of the Times: The untractable Spirit of Lewdness is sunk into gentle Gallantry, and Obscenity itself is grown effeminate.

"But what Vice hath lost in Coarseness of Expression, she hath gained in a more easy and general Admittance: In ancient Days, bare and impudent Obscenity, like a common Woman of the Town, was confined to Brothels: Whereas the Double-Entendre, like a modern fine lady, is now admitted into the best Company; while her transparent Covering of Words, like a thin fashionable Gawze delicately thrown across, discloses, while it seems to veil, her Nakedness of Thought [pp. 44–45]."

at achieving more precise meaning by more exact definition of terms. But in his sport with possible connotations of "nose," Sterne clearly demonstrates that, given some knowledge of human preconceptions, one has only to manipulate the context in order to manipulate the meaning. Protests of "one word —one meaning" simply serve to alert the reader to the possibility of *double entendre*. The Slawkenbergian story about the man with the long nose who so fascinated the people of Strasburg that they could think of nothing else, serves not only to titillate Sterne's readers, but also provides an excellent example of the futility of pedantry, and, even more, of its danger. The learned ones of Strasburg did nothing to alleviate the "nose-madness" of the townspeople. They merely facilitated the downfall of the town.

At the heart of the struggle against the perverse misapplication of intelligence, in other words, against learning without wisdom, as Aubrey Williams has pointed out in his study of the *Dunciad*, lay a concern with the means, use, ends, and limits of human knowledge.[9] One of the principal fields of contention, then as now, was the problem of communication. How can one best convey knowledge once it is obtained? The scientist and the logician, more interested in matter than manner, tended to denounce the art of rhetoric as mere self-display. For the humanist, on the other hand, rhetoric, ideally, was the communication of wisdom. Pope, like Swift, attacked the sort of empty verbalism which rhetoric had become as well as the "dunces" who, instead of learning to know themselves, either fastened on external factual knowledge, or sought knowledge beyond man's capabilities, and who were, in fact, knowledge-proud, lacking the humility which comes only through self-knowledge. The humanist-orator, then, is distinguished from the narrow metaphysician and scientist by his ability to put knowledge to use, to communicate wisdom. Father Shandy, that "excellent natural philosopher . . . much

[9]*Pope's Dunciad: A Study of its Meaning* (London, 1955), pp. 105–10.

given to close reasoning upon the smallest matters," is a brilliant illustration of one who possesses knowledge but not wisdom. He is so lost in speculative philosophy that he has no thought of the genuine needs of those under his charge— his wife and sons. His theoretical concern for their welfare is so compelling that he has lost touch with the concrete reality of their human wants and desires. Yet the "elements of Logick and Rhetorick" are "blended up in him" (I, xix, 52). He is eloquent, but he has no real knowledge to communicate—only eccentric speculations. However, even if he had attended Cambridge (Sterne's Alma Mater), he would have learned, according to Tristram, only the names of his rhetorical tools, not their genuine significance.

Father Shandy has knowledge, of a sort, but little compassion and almost no tenderness of heart. Uncle Toby is tender-hearted enough, but lacks knowledge of the world. His modesty is "unparalleled," not in regard to words (since he has very little choice of them), but in regard to things. Toby has a "female nicety," the "inward cleanliness of mind and fancy" associated with that sex; but this is a "cleanliness" that Tristram often apparently overlooks in his female readers if one can judge by the numerous questionable passages included for their delectation. As a matter of fact, as the narrative progresses, we find that even the "innocent" Toby can appreciate the point of Dr. Slop's innuendo on "curtins and horn-works." In any event, Uncle Toby is not an orator. When Walter Shandy proclaims that the life of a family is nothing compared to an hypothesis which may bring one closer to truth, and that, in the forum of science, there is no such thing as murder, only death, Uncle Toby can but whistle "Lillabullero" in answer. Toby's hobby-horse originates in his inability to communicate, to express himself clearly, to explain to his visitors how he came by his wound. He seeks the help of "things"—visual aid in the form of a map—to replace words. " 'Twas not by ideas, ——by heaven! his life was put in jeopardy by words" (II, ii,

87). Toby, then, becomes, in his way, a virtuoso, a pedant, acquiring knowledge not, as he had originally intended, in order to communicate it in the form of accounts of how he obtained his wound, but rather to gather, in a sort of mania, more and more facts about fortifications, not quite as ends in themselves, but as a sort of escape from such concrete problems of everyday human existence as those posed by the Widow Wadman. "Endless is the Search of Truth!" comments Tristram, and then goes on to show that what Toby is engaged in is pursuit of "phantom knowledge," not of wisdom in the humanist sense.

Father Shandy shares the "common-place infirmity of the greatest mathematicians! working with might and main at the demonstration, and so wasting all their strength upon it, that they have none left in them to draw the corollary, to do good with." He is a minute philosopher whose hypotheses tend to assimilate everything to themselves as proper nourishment. His "rhetoric and conduct" are "at perpetual handy-cuffs." "Inconsistent soul that man is!" says Tristram, "languishing under wounds, which he has the power to heal!—his whole life a contradiction to his knowledge!" (III, xxi, 203). Toby, in his turn, though he will not hurt a fly, is more concerned with his *idée fixe* than with the labour pains of his sister-in-law. Tristram, in fact, makes a distinction between Toby's *moral* character and his *hobby-horsical* character. Toby will spend any amount on his hobby-horse, and justifies the expense by contending that it is for the good of the nation. But his "campaigns," in one sense, display a desire to reduce large matters (such as wars) to small, manoeuvrable, and relatively innocent symbols. As occupational therapy they are, as the practical Trim foresaw, extremely effective, so effective that they become, for Toby, almost the whole of life. The tendency to treat human beings as "things," evident in Uncle Toby's dehumanized version of war, is a dominant strand in the book.

From the first, we are made aware of the mechanistic basis of Father Shandy's theories. He prefers to reduce life to clockwork. From his vantage point the backslidings of Venus in her orbit are comparable to the backslidings of Tristram's Aunt Dinah. Both are part of a system.

One of the prime jokes in *Tristram Shandy* is the strange working of cause and effect. Human destinies are often curiously determined. Tristram, that pawn of fate, is a flagrant example of the severe limitations which are by the very nature of things placed on individual free will. A good deal of the novel is given up to accounts of how Tristram's destiny is determined even before the time of his conception. There is the carefully drafted legal document concerning Mrs. Shandy's right to bear her children in London, which in fact (because, one notes, of benign Uncle Toby's concern that his brother should not be duped) has the exact opposite effect to that intended and leads straight to Tristram's difficult birth in Shandy Hall. This is just one of many illustrations of human inability to shape the future by taking thought, by attempting to plan like an omniscient being. The by-play about the baptizing of infants before birth "par le moyen d'une petite canulle" (I, xx, 62) is another example of the ways in which the destinies of humans may be effectively shaped even before they leave the womb. The comedy lies (as it does in the case of the legal phraseology of the marriage settlement) in the disparity between the desiccated tone and the human implications. In its striving for objectivity and impartiality, such language denies the very humanity it seeks to treat with impeccable fairness. Whenever he tries to act with complete disinterest (in a god-like way to sit in judgment) man inevitably treats his fellow humans as things—as mechanisms. Father Shandy tries to take a "scientific" approach to human affairs, looks for "impersonal" laws governing personal relations. Throughout we have the irony of his failure to systematize human inconsequentiality, but a failure often resulting from forces (such as a falling window or a pair of forceps) just as impersonal as his own systems.

IV

In volume two Tristram makes jocular, but significant, reference to the decay of eloquence since classical times. Ironically, he uses as an illustration of the classical facility with language the possibility of reinforcing the word by producing the very object mentioned from beneath the orator's cloak at the strategic moment. And the example given of modern incompetence in matters oratorical is not one concerning a failure of words, but rather Dr. Slop's fumbling attempt to provide concrete illustration of his words, an attempt which goes awry when he unfortunately seizes from his green baize bag not only the forceps with which he aids delivery of the child but also the squirt used in administering pre-natal baptism (III, xv, 186). In the misplaced "Author's Preface" which appears in this same volume, Sterne speaks out on behalf of concrete illustrations as a readier means of communication than "tall, opake words" which come "betwixt your own and your reader's conception."

"Writing," Tristram argues early in volume two, "when properly managed (as you may be sure I think mine is), is but a different name for conversation." Throughout *Tristram Shandy*, Sterne obviously tries to give the impression that he is really carrying on what amounts to a lively conversation with his readers, allowing them, from time to time, opportunities to reply. But for all the apparent attempt to produce dialogue, the book is for the most part monologue. The "dear Madam," or "fair reader," or even "Sir Critick" addressed by Sterne is frequently a straw horse set up as part of the novel's devious rhetoric. Sterne's technique is close to that of the pedagogue, or the preacher: extended commentary on a text, dialogue with a book, which, like Sterne's reader, has its answers provided for it.

The novel is the art form of the printing press and is written by an individual sitting alone in his study for the eyes of another individual sitting alone in his armchair. For all his talk of elocution and oratory, Sterne thinks of his book as something to be *seen*, not heard. He is conscious of the way the words *look* on the page. He is constantly supplementing them with such visual devices as asterisks, pointing fingers, and black and mottled pages. He even attempts to diagram the course of his various volumes. A Lockean concept of the human intellect naturally gives rise to a distrust of words, which are, after all, a rather inadequate substitution of sounds for "ideas." These "ideas" are originally, in the pre-speech phase, pictures or images projected on the screen of the mind.[10] The one page in Sterne's book which "Malice will not blacken, and which Ignorance cannot misrepresent," is the one left

[10]In *The Concept of Mind* (London, 1949), pp. 158–59, Gilbert Ryle describes the Lockean concept of a mental world whose contents are self-luminous, and in which "consciousness" functions in the same way as light in the Newtonian universe. In terms of such a model, the mind is thought of as a region to be observed, very much in the way that we observe the world around us. We *look* within in order to *see*—we do not soliloquize like Hamlet, nor do we listen to an inner voice. The world within, however luminous, is a silent world. See also Ernest Tuveson, *The Imagination as a Means of Grace*, p. 21: "Locke does, to be sure, recognize that simple ideas of sensation come in through all five (and more) senses, but only sight is significant for the understanding faculty, for thought is seeing."

Walter Ong, too, has called attention to the fact that with the transfer of significance from the "word" heard to the "thing" seen, knowledge is in a sense depersonalized. In *Ramus: Method, and the Decay of Dialogue* (Cambridge, Mass., 1958), p. 318, he notes: ". . . the Ramist reworking of dialectic and rhetoric furthered the elimination of sound and voice from man's understanding of the intellectual world and helped create within the human spirit itself the silences of a spatialized universe." The ideal becomes "objectivity"—the removal, as much as possible, of the human element. (Significantly, the ideal, in the novel, also became in our time the "removal" of the author, as much as possible, from his own work.) See also Father Ong's "A Dialectic of Aural and Objective Correlatives," *Essays in Criticism*, VIII (1958), 166–81.

blank for the purpose of allowing readers to draw their own picture of the "concupiscible" Widow Wadman. And the widow, incidentally, is probably the most effective "orator" in the book, with the possible exception of Trim. She is only too successful in communicating her amorous feelings to Uncle Toby—without, one notes, the use of words. Her principal means of "speech" is her eye.

Book IV of Pope's *Dunciad* paints a picture of Chaos ruled by the "uncreating" Word, the babble of the Dunce. *Tristram Shandy*, in its way, is an extension of Pope's vision. It gives an account of human life not as a tale told by an idiot but as the story of a Cock and a Bull. Here is Tristram, the self-conscious Dunce, writing a book apparently modelled on the usual Grub Street productions of the time,[11] but, like Swift in his somewhat similar enterprise in parts of *A Tale of a Tub*, producing instead a graphic description of the times. Here is the sort of fare the reading public wants, complete with that little ironic fillip of self-awareness which provides the necessary comment on that public and on the world which it dominates. It is a world in which the mechanical means of communication are becoming more and more efficient; while, at the same time, the articulateness, the ability to communicate, is steadily declining. Knowledge is on the upswing—wisdom on the downgrade.

Tristram Shandy is one more engagement in the perpetual war between wits and "dunces" but Sterne's role in battle is rather different from that of Swift or Pope. His approach is much more tentative, his attack much less bitter—presumably because his positive beliefs are much less surely held. Swift's writings "express" ideas, or communicate firmly held points of view, by attacking opposing ideas. Sterne, on the other hand, is seeking to reveal states of mind. Swift attacked the Grub Street hack by parodying his style; Pope sallied against the pedantic dunce by burlesquing his method; and Sterne,

---

[11]See Wayne C. Booth, "The Self-Conscious Narrator in Comic Fiction before *Tristram Shandy*," *PMLA*, LXVII (1952).

in his turn, donned cap and bells in order to show up foolishness by playing the fool. Unlike the others, however, the jester
Sterne was willing to admit that he was able to act his part
so well because he was, in fact, himself a trifle foolish. This,
of course, accounts for the tendency of readers to evince more
affection for Sterne the man than for either Swift or Pope.
It also accounts for the tendency to take what he says much
less seriously, for, by assuming the mask of fool, one not only
avoids a certain amount of responsibility for one's actions, one
also denies the credit for one's "accidental wit."[12]

[12]A. E. Dyson provides a penetrating discussion of Sterne's role as
narrator in *Tristram Shandy* in "Sterne: The Novelist as Jester," *Critical
Quarterly*, IV (1962), 309–20. He comments on Sterne's peculiar genius
in the relationship he establishes with his readers—far closer to friendship,
he feels, than any other novelist ever comes.

Tristram as Clown

SATIRE characteristically implies an ideal and often attacks this world (and perhaps its Maker) because it cannot conceivably ever attain to such ideality. This accounts for the savagery of much satire. But comedy finally implies acceptance of the world—not as ideal, certainly, but as necessary—and stresses in its contrived happy endings the possibility of at least limited human happiness, provided one does not take oneself too seriously or attempt in too radical a manner to obtain immunity from life's inevitable unpleasantnesses. Comedy eschews the heroic, preferring the mock-heroic, and is willing to settle (at least in this world) for less than the ideal, seeing man as by nature ungodlike, unheroic, and his salvation as lying in his ability to recognize and accept, perhaps even welcome, his human limitations. Comedy, then, can certainly be seen as therapeutic (or cathartic) in the Aristotelian sense. It enables us to bear our troubles by teaching us to laugh at them and ourselves. It stresses the fact that man's capacity for happiness depends to a large extent on his vulnerability to the slings and arrows of outrageous fortune.

VOLUMES ONE AND TWO

I

Tristram is the author as comic hero—as clown or jester. From the very opening pages he warns the reader that he, the author, has himself been marred at his beginning. The reader has been duly alerted. But, aware of the long standing tradition of the wise fool—the ironic praiser of folly—he reads on not only to be amused but also perhaps to be enlightened. As Tristram gabbles on facetiously about the homunculus and its hazardous journey, he attempts to deny that his purpose is levity; he associates himself instead with the "minutest philosophers," the scientists of his day. And, by drawing a parallel between the homunculus and the human being that it may become, he likens its journey to the womb to man's journey through life. (The conventional view of "life as a journey" is given a number of unconventional twists in *Tristram Shandy* and *A Sentimental Journey*.) The homunculus, too, becomes a sort of melancholy clown, subject to all the ills of the flesh. The underlying parallel is between the birth of a child and the birth of a work of prose fiction. The reader is frequently to wonder in the ensuing pages whether the author is duly minding what he is doing as he creates his book. And the clown-author of course deliberately plays the role of scatter-brain who cannot keep his mind on the progress of his narrative for more than a page or two together.

If one conceives of comedy as "a contrast between the ugly, buffoonish clown who is the central figure, and the norms he implies by violating them,"[1] presumably Tristram as incompetent author implies a writer with more obvious qualifications as a story-teller. Thus he is writing not so much an anti-novel

[1] Albert Cook, *The Dark Voyage and the Golden Mean* (Cambridge, Mass., 1949), p. 39. Ruth Nevo in "Towards a Theory of Comedy," *JAAC*, XXI (1963), 327–32, interestingly discusses the role of the clown-hero in comic works.

as an affirmation of serious artistic norms. This possible "meaning" for Tristram, however, raises a number of problems, notably the kind of "ideal" Sterne might have had in mind, or, more pragmatically, the kind of work his audience might have accepted as the "norm" in relation to which *Tristram Shandy* could be seen as ludicrous. There is another possible interpretation: Tristram as clown-author draws attention to the very real obstacles which lie in the path of artistic accomplishment, emphasizes the human frailties of even the greatest author, and creates a critical awareness in the reader of some of the goals which authors have sought; in the process of all this he is perhaps calling into question the attainability of these goals, or even the desirability of attaining them.

In the early chapters the clowning technique consists principally in burlesquing the concern with minutiae which marks so many novels of the "life and times" school. Tristram circumstantially traces his beginnings, pedantically settling on the very night of his conception and giving apparently infallible (partially documentary) proof for his certainty as to the exact date.[2] All this is accomplished with the dash and poise of a conjuror producing rabbits from a hat. The comic tone of the work is being carefully established. The world into which Tristram is brought forth, the one into which his book is launched, is the world as experienced by the clown: "scurvy and disasterous," "One of the vilest worlds that ever was made," and yet not one marked by "any great or signal evil," but a place in which the "small HERO" has been subjected to "a set of . . . pitiful misadventures and cross accidents." This is, then, the traditional world of the comic hero.

Tristram is soon affirming that he is "not a wise man," and

---

[2]Maurice Johnson has discovered an interesting precursor to Sterne in this aspect of his comedy; see "A Comic Homunculus before *Tristram Shandy*," *The Library Chronicle*, XXXI (1965), 83–90. See also Louis Landa, "The Shandean Homunculus: The Background of Sterne's 'Little Gentleman'," in *Restoration and Eighteenth-Century Literature*, ed. Carroll Camden (Chicago, 1963).

that he is "a mortal of so little consequence in the world, it is not much matter what I do," even though he has previously hinted that he may possess a little more wisdom than appears upon his outside, and has stated categorically that his "life and opinions are likely to make some noise in the world" and "be no less read than the *Pilgrim's Progress* itself." The ludicrous comparison of his book with Bunyan's is obviously intended to underline the traditional joke about the clown's wisdom, but in proclaiming later on his "little consequence," he is not denying the possibility of his being capable of wise sayings; rather he is re-stressing his wisdom, since he has seen and accepted himself for what he is. In this sense, he is superior to Lords A, B, C, D, and so on, who are completely at the mercy of their various hobby-horses.

The clown-hero is throughout indirectly characterizing himself, skilfully constructing his persona. But as clown he can only *imply* a norm, a set of positives. However, in his descriptions of others and in his illustrative anecdotes concerning them he can be more direct in his praise and blame. Significantly, the first person he draws a full-scale portrait of is Parson Yorick; ironically, an idealized portrait of Sterne himself. We seem to have in Yorick the closest thing to a "norm" against which to test the clown-hero's world. The most serious pages of the opening chapters are devoted to him, and we are given a fairly clear impression of his attributes. He is modest, witty, unselfish, thinking constantly of his parishioners, but he is not without his human foibles. He is related, albeit distantly, to Shakespeare's "wise fools"; he is indiscreetly frank in his denunciation of evil, yet as naïve in some of his attitudes as Don Quixote, with whom he is firmly associated from the beginning by means of his horse.[3] Chapter twelve of volume

[3]In a sense, Don Quixote is one of the controlling "norms" of this topsy-turvy world. Tristram notes quite explicitly his high regard for "the peerless knight of *La Mancha*" (I, x, 22). What Don Quixote represents as "norm" is by no means easy to state simply; see Oscar Mandel, "The Function of the Norm in *Don Quixote*," *MP*, vv (1957–58), 154–63.

one, with its account of the death of Yorick, is to a certain extent a serious discussion of the plight of the jester. Like Don Quixote, he must eventually succumb, disabused and disillusioned, though he will have at least one faithful friend by his side (Eugenius) and at least one chronicler who cares enough to tell his story. But the pathos of the death scene is not dwelt on. We are reminded that jesters too are mortal; but then the story rebounds, and Parson Yorick, miraculously, is very much alive again. We have been assured that he has gone to a wiser judge and that those who live on will frequently pay their respects at his graveside, repeating with feeling his Shakespearean epitaph.

Now, Tristram, perhaps a trifle more sober in manner since his recollection of Yorick's end, proceeds to expatiate on the difficulties faced by the "historiographer." As clown-author he is to be subjected to many and various frustrations. But he bears up under these, as befits his role, with considerable equanimity. Take the case of the article in his mother's marriage settlement. This is a piece of documentation he must find if he is to tell his story properly and substantiate his version of it. He anticipates endless trouble in locating it, because such is the recalcitrant nature of his world. However, he rejoices that he came upon it "before he had read a day and a half straight forwards." But "a day and a half" of such verbiage as he now proceeds to display for the enlightenment of the reader is surely no mean obstacle. The reader, given (Tristram claims) only the gist of the matter, is at the point of tossing the book aside (or skipping to the end of the passage) when Tristram, with exquisite timing, sums up the relevant portions of the document "in three words" and picks up his narrative again. The basic comic pattern is a familiar one: the ludicrous contrast between the ponderous legal terminology (skilfully parodied by Sterne) designed to seal off loopholes (that is, misunderstandings) in the message communicated and the crystal clarity of Tristram's comic reduction of that message to simple English. But above and beyond this is the reader's awareness of the mocking voice of Tristram reading this tortuous prose aloud (prose that is really composed to be seen not heard), emphasizing the pains the writer-cum-scholar must take in the interests of his art, and, at the same time, inadvertently revealing the sort of marriage relationship which produced Tristram, the small hero who is now its historian. This is a marriage evidently built on mutual suspicion, rather than mutual trust; it is a legal contract, a business transaction. And the result of all this laborious legal machination is, of course, one more discomfiting pre-natal blow at the clown-hero.

II

During the discussion about the marriage contract we have been given a portrait of Father Shandy to set beside that of Yorick. He, too, is a comic figure, but his obstinacy, his egotism, his lack of human sympathy, all mark him off clearly from the Cervantean Yorick. Obviously he is cast in the part of chief belabourer of the clown-author, his main begetter, and the main begetter of his various ludicrous misfortunes—just as, paradoxically, Tristram as author is the creator of this father who figures so prominently in the narrative. Thus the clown contrives his own discomfitures for the sake of the laughter his antics can win from his audience. And the audience, in laughing, rejects the folly it finds amusing, but accepts the clown who, in portraying it, has brought the release of laughter. (A satirist would not be accepted in this way; the laughter he calls forth is nervous and perhaps bitter, and he himself is not its butt. The members of his audience have the uncomfortable feeling that they themselves are being portrayed as clowns.)

The pattern of misadventure for the clown-narrator is set from the beginning: the unfortunate *contretemps* of his conception is soon followed by the forebodings connected with his mother's enforced confinement in the country, and Father Shandy's elaborate theorizing about names which, as is made clear by the name of the book, has resulted in the very name he most despised being given to his son. Thus the apparent disorder of the book—the projection of the clown as author— would seem to provide proof of the validity of Walter Shandy's various theories. But inasmuch as the clown can convince us of wisdom underlying his foolery, he casts serious doubts on Walter's hypotheses. Walter, too, like the traditional clown, is a victim of cross purposes. His most carefully planned designs for ordering the future come to naught, apparently through the crass casualty of the nature of things, but also because he is not very adept at turning theory into practice.

Tristram as narrator (as was noted in the last chapter) frequently invites audience participation, as in the case of the inattentive lady who did not realize that Tristram's mother was not a papist. Most members of the reading audience must, of course, plead equally guilty with this lady in their failure to grasp the implications of Tristram's having to be born before he could be christened. The charge of inattentiveness is ludicrously exaggerated, but there is left in the reader's mind the suggestion (duly reinforced from time to time) that much of Tristram's foolery may be more significant than it appears on the surface. For example, the main point at issue in the reported discussion of the Doctors of the Sorbonne is the possible damnation of an unborn child, and a good deal of Tristram's commentary in the early stages of his "life and opinions" has a similar focus: to what extent is a child's destiny determined by the apparently inconsequential actions of its parents; to what extent do even well-intentioned efforts of theirs affect the child for the worse? In Tristram's small world his parents play roles comparable to those assigned to the gods in Greek mythology. Their petty bickering, their intransigence, are the shaping factors which determine his future. His absurd family becomes a paradigm for an absurd world.[4] But—and here is an element which marks his work as comic rather than satiric—he accepts all this in good part. He obviously enjoys the foibles of his parents, just as he expects his audience to enjoy his antics as clown. And there is always the possibility, constantly hinted at, that the world only *seems* absurd, just as Tristram's clowning only *seems* to have no point. Tristram's plight viewed differently would be pathetic; but this is not how it is viewed. It is comic. And the essence of the comic world, even at its most disorderly, is its dependence upon, and its implied affirmation of, its eventual return to order.

Tristram makes fun of the Doctors' deliberations. Spoken by the clown, their serious report sounds like magnificent tomfoolery. Their theories are lumped with Father Shandy's. Tristram's main purpose is to emphasize the dehumanized language in which the Doctors discuss what for the individuals concerned would be heart-rending sorrows. Like Swift's modest proposer, by abstracting themselves from particular cases, they achieve a seemingly objective neutrality which, in the mouth of the clown-narrator, becomes ludicrously inhumane. The *reductio ad absurdum* of his closing suggestion for the extension of the ruling to all homunculi emphasizes not so much the apparent absurdity of the doctrine as the insensitivity of its language. The report is followed immediately by the account of the insensitivity of Walter and Toby to Mrs. Shandy's impending labour. But the account is only just begun before the mention of Toby sends Tristram off on a long digression describing his character and his hobby-horse. So Tristram, too, is ironically exposed as insensitive, as more interested in the birth pangs of his narrative than in those experienced by his mother upon his own coming into being.

[4]See Ernest H. Lockridge, "A Vision of the Sentimental Absurd: Sterne and Camus," *Sewanee Review*, LXXII (1964), 652–67.

Tristram's digressions have been much discussed,[5] and frequently his own justification of them has been accepted at face value. He asserts that his work is progressive as well as digressive, that he is delineating Uncle Toby's character at the very moment when he seems to be straying from this purpose to talk of Aunt Dinah's indiscretion; but this is the rationalization of the clown-author and he habitually protests too much. Few of his digressions can actually be justified as aspects of characterization or plot development, but they are, nevertheless, an essential part of the book's comic structure. The garrulous clown characterizes himself as narrator by his tendency to digress, and by a queer kind of almost accidental logic his digressions do add significant dimensions to his clownish rhetoric. In one sense he is parodying the hack writers of his time. But parody entails critical awareness of the thing parodied. Some digressions are as inconsequential as they seem; they are purely comic in intent, designed in part to keep the reader guessing. Others are most revealing. The digression on digressions (I, xxii, 72–73) adds nothing to our understanding of Uncle Toby's character, and not much to our understanding of Sterne's narrative method. But the explicit parallel between book and machine which Tristram makes use of here (while conjuring up visions of a Rube Goldberg creation when applied to Tristram's book) introduces once more another traditional aspect of the clown's role, that of man as mechanism. It is the tendency of the clown to be somewhat less than human, to think of a story concerning flesh-and-blood individuals in terms of mechanical manipulation, to think of himself as author as a sort of superior mechanic—this is what is laughable, particularly when the end result is anything but a smoothly running piece of clockwork. Involved here is the whole effort to reduce art to a set of principles, to a formula. The spirit manifested by Tristram in this portion of the book

[5]See, for example, William Bowman Piper, "Tristram Shandy's Digressive Artistry," *SEL*, I (1961), 65–76.

is the very one he has previously castigated in the Doctors of the Sorbonne and in his parents' marriage deed.

The digressive chapters are examples of the comic use of *non sequitur*. The defence of digression in chapter twenty-two is followed immediately by a chapter which begins "very nonsensically" with a facetious discussion of Momus's proposed glass in the human breast. The subject is a profoundly serious one: the relation of soul to body, and, by implication, the nature of the soul and how it may be known. With an appropriate flourish this is connected with what has gone before by its being used as a springboard to leap, in the next chapter, into an account of Tristram's method of characterizing his Uncle Toby by means of his hobby-horse. We are amused by the clown-author's nimbleness, by his ability to tie together the seemingly most irrelevant matters, but we should not be unaware that, in the process of writing nonsensically, Tristram has skilfully drawn attention to what is really involved in the creation of a character in a work of fiction. The author is in effect gazing into the innermost recesses of the character's being and reporting what he finds there. He is assaying his "soul." And in this task Tristram has deliberately denied the efficacy of "mechanical help"; particularly he has eschewed methods which are grossly materialistic in their accounts of man's nature, methods which describe him largely in terms of his excretions and retentions.

But what of Tristram's own technique? How seriously, again, are we to take his glib defence of the hobby-horse as a sound guide to a man's soul? We cannot help noting that his description of the relationship between hobby-horse and man makes use of an analogy with the interaction of electrified bodies, an analogy which says in effect that the hobby-horse *is* the man because the man becomes full of the hobby-horse. This whole matter of hobby-horses stems in a direct line from Cervantes and Quixotic monomanias generally, including the Jonsonian comedy of humours. The underlying premise is that the eccentricity is in a sense the whole man. Uncle Toby is the most Cervantic of all Sterne's characters, and our attitude to him, like our attitude to the Don himself, is not easy to assess. Toby is a figure of fun, and yet he is presented most sympathetically. Like Quixote he is at times a buffoon, and yet we cannot help developing an affection for him. His hobby-horse evolves out of his desire to speed his recovery from his wound. It has a therapeutic function. It stems also from his desire to communicate, to tell his story. Thus his motivation is very similar to Tristram's, who also seeks to escape from melancholy thoughts of his misfortunes by setting them comically on paper for the delectation of his audience; and, like his Uncle Toby, he seeks to communicate, and finds the task a difficult and frustrating one.

Toby, however, is "freed" from a world of sad explanations by his hobby-horse; Tristram is plunged into the midst of an endless endeavour to tell of his various wounds—the very effort to communicate providing, though, in his case, the escape from "the spleen." The "Lockean" Tristram (and one must ask the same questions about his Lockean clowning as one asks about his espousal of the digression and the hobby-horse) is most conscious of the "unsteady uses of words" which give Uncle Toby such trouble. Thus he can sympathize readily with his uncle's frustrations in his attempts to describe the siege of Namur to his visitors. But his sympathies do not prevent him from straying into a discussion of Locke's theories of perception in order to explain "the true cause of confusion in my uncle *Toby's* discourse" by showing "what it did *not* arise from." Tristram, clown and pedant *par excellence*, cannot resist his thrust at the academic approach, even though in the process he becomes an example of what he ridicules.

Uncle Toby's recovery from the effects of his wound depends, we are told, on his being able to talk without emotion about the subject closest to his heart. He must objectify it— turn it into something else which he can observe dispassionately. This, too, then, is what Tristram is doing. His book, like Toby's model battle fields, is an abstraction from bitter experience which enables him to cope with the harsh facts of life by transforming them into manipulable symbols. It is only when life refuses to be reduced to manageable proportions that Tristram and Toby occasionally find themselves unable to cope. Their characteristic defence in such cases is an even more rigorous application of their particular method of controlling life's dynamism. Both men are aspects of the clown.

Toby's recovery is by no means immediate; he has to tame his hobby-horse before he can ride it comfortably. In his first excitement, he strives for knowledge much too hard and becomes lost in a maze of mathematics. Tristram is led to apostrophize the dangers to health inherent in such a rigorous search for "this bewitching phantom"—likening Knowledge to a serpent and thus conjuring up visions of the primal Fall and Toby as Adam in motley. (Toby's Eve, the Widow Wadman, who has not yet made her appearance, represents knowledge of a rather less mathematical kind and fires from her eyes projectiles perhaps more lethal than the one which levelled Toby at Namur.) What saves Toby at this point is, first, his return to the more concrete science of fortifications, and, second, and most important, Corporal Trim's inspired suggestion that he conduct his investigations much more empirically by constructing actual laboratory specimens of batteries, saps, ditches, palisadoes, and so on. Involved in this is the return to the country estate at Shandy, a comic version of the primal Garden, perhaps. Tristram's attitude to Toby is indulgent. He thinks of him as almost child-like: guileless, extremely sympathetic, and rather stupid—though with the flashes of insight that come unexpectedly in children.

The narrative now returns abruptly to the conversation between Walter and Toby which was interrupted many pages previous to allow for the insertion of a character sketch of Uncle Toby. The conversation itself, which takes place by the parlour fire-side, had been occasioned by the disturbance in the rooms above which accompanied Tristram's impending arrival. Typically, Walter Shandy's first reaction to news of his wife's condition is to send for Dr. Slop so that his own interests (and particularly his own pet theories about child-birth) might be looked after. The conversation between the brothers, like the conversation between Tristram and his readers (of which of course it forms a part), is fraught with uncertainties and pitfalls. At this point Uncle Toby is attempt-ing to be the voice of reason: he suggests ringing for Obadiah to learn what the commotion is about (rather than speculating idly as Walter seems intent on doing); he suggests reasons for Mrs. Shandy's apparently perverse insistence on being attended by a midwife rather than the male *accoucheur*, Dr. Slop. But his "reasons" are "unreasonable" as far as Walter is concerned; Walter, like Tristram, thinks of Toby as impos-sibly naïve in practical matters, especially those concerning women. (It is at this point [II, vii, 101], incidentally, that we first hear of the affair with the Widow Wadman which is to form the closing episode of the book.) Toby attributes to Mrs. Shandy his own modesty, only to be ridiculed by Walter, and guyed by narrator Tristram who, by his equivocal method of presenting Toby's suggestion that Mrs. Shandy might have some misgivings about a man midwife coming near her at this juncture, toys with the ambiguities of his possibly incomplete sentence. Tristram's bawdiness has hereto-fore been rather more subtle. But now, having established his role as clown quite firmly, and having attained a sense of rapport with his audience, he apparently feels he can be more outspoken. At the same time, he makes quite clear that the various gaps and ambiguities which are to follow in his narrative may be interpreted in several ways. He alerts the reader to possible indecencies, at the same time implicating him in their recognition. The bawdy joke is as old as comedy itself. Tristram as clown-author is again in this aspect of his foolery following well-established tradition. The clown characteristically plays with dynamite,[6] shocking his audience into laughter by his irreverent treatment of themes highly charged with emotional overtones: frequently in Tristram's case (as with many other clowns) the themes of religion and sex.

III

The discussion between Toby and Walter ends as inconsequentially as most other discussions in the book. In this it is almost a paradigm of the book's structure, with its halting progress and rapid changes of direction and eventual fizzling out into vague promises of being continued in a later volume. The interruption this time is Obadiah's return with Dr. Slop and the ensuing comic interchanges between Tristram and his hypothetical critics over the nature of narrative realism in works of prose fiction. Tristram, once more a burlesque Lockean, tosses in learned allusions to "the idea of duration and of its simple modes" (II, viii, 103) and goads his reader by giving a slightly distorted account of the narrative sequence. (He suggests that the sending of Obadiah on his quest was reported *before* the long digression concerning Uncle Toby rather than at the end of it.) The clown has a vested interest in theories about time and its fictive representation since, as entertainer, he undertakes to pass the time, or at least to make the inevitable passage of human time more bearable by rendering it comic. No one is more aware of fleeting time than, paradoxically, Tristram himself, and this awareness grows as his narrative develops. The references to time and mutability become more frequent and more pointed, until the closing sections in which the clown hero reverts once more to facetious re-creation of time long past.

The Hogarthian figure (accompanied by a reference to Hogarth, II, ix, 104) who now makes his entrance is a visitor

[6]As Ruth Nevo puts it in "Towards a Theory of Comedy."

from the world of farce. His "rencounter" with Obadiah outside Shandy Hall, and its muddy consequences, are "pure"
slapstick. We are left in no doubt as to how seriously we are
to take this man midwife who is, in addition, a papist. (His
insistence on crossing himself during his collision with Obadiah is largely responsible for his falling into the mud.) It is
understandable that a clown-narrator should describe a world
peopled with clowns. He sees all of the characters, even the
semi-idealized Yorick, as suffering from ludicrous deficiencies
comparable to his own—though none except Yorick is able
to carry off these flaws as capably as he, the observer and
interpreter of this world, is able to do. Of all the alternative
clown figures, Dr. Slop is given the roughest treatment. He
makes his entrance "unwiped, unappointed, unanealed, with
all his stains and blotches on him," and yet this is the man
to whose fumbling hands Father Shandy is willing to entrust
the coming of baby Tristram into the world. (The overtones
of theological controversy are as thick about Dr. Slop as the
mire in which he has been immersed. His ungodlike "hinder
parts" are observed "without mental reservation," and his
obstetrical contrivances are called "instruments of salvation
and deliverance.")

Dr. Slop is deposited in all the majesty of mud in the back-
parlour and the reader is invited to imagine his explanation
of his appearance and the subsequent steps taken to clean
him up and seat him once more in the parlour to await
Obadiah's arrival with his "green bays" instrument bag. So
we are aware of Tristram as stage-manager and scene-setter
as we focus on the ensuing conversation among the brothers
Shandy and the man midwife, a conversation which is in
fact an exercise in cross purposes. Toby, astride his hobby-
horse, collides with Walter, trying to get astride his, just as
explosively as Obadiah and Dr. Slop came together outside
Shandy Hall. And it is Walter who is unseated and spattered
in this collision. His temper gets the better of him. He de-

nounces the whole science of fortification, claims obsession with it has rendered Toby oblivious to everything else, including the fact that Mrs. Shandy is in the pains of labour (something about which he himself up to this point had shown no concern). But in response Toby has only to look wistfully at his brother to soften his heart and effect an emotional reconciliation.

Meanwhile, the jester-narrator makes use of Dr. Slop to keep the situation from becoming maudlin. Slop puns about "curtins and horn-works" very much in the manner of Tristram, while Walter and Toby react in their individual ways to this breach in decorum. Slop here makes the remarks usually associated with masculine conversation; he shows his wit, and his "manliness," by his ability to jest about the serious business of sex. Walter and Toby obviously deviate from this stereotyped pattern, though on other occasions Walter adheres to it. In matters of sex, Toby is always solemnly unsophisticated. He explains pedantically that "curtins" are not bed-curtains and that "horn-works" have nothing to do with cuckoldom. He has fortified himself against this dynamic element in human nature by immersing himself in the science of fortifications. (Significantly, the crux of the book consists of a detailed account of the occasion on which his Maginot line was temporarily breached by the heavy artillery of the Widow Wadman.) It is in this very chapter that the notorious anecdote about his treatment of the fly occurs. To some extent Toby is a comic version of the saint, a saint whose "religion" is the science of warfare. He is so engrossed in this science that he seems completely oblivious to its cost in human suffering, despite the fact that he is inordinately sympathetic by nature, as the fly incident is designed to show. Presumably, an impregnable fortress would prevent loss of life by repelling all invaders (a tactic for the prevention of war by no means without its advocates in our own century). But Toby is represented as interested in knowledge for its own sake, as a sort of therapy, rather than in any practical application of it. He plays at war in order to undo the damage which war has done to him in the form of the wound on his groin. Like comic figures generally, then, he is a scapegoat who arouses the laughter of the audience in part because they can thus vicariously laugh at some of their own foibles. He is the comic fisher-king of this fable, the maimed figure who is sacrificed to restore the fertility of the land. Like his great predecessor Quixote, he is directly related to the stereotypes of the comedy of humours, but, like the Don also, he transcends these narrow limits by becoming a lovable human being in the Chaplinesque mode.

Walter is something else again. His fence against life is the realm of pure abstraction. In this realm, theory is ostensibly designed to lend order to the flux of existence. In fact, of course, his theories are of as little practical use as Toby's model forts, perhaps even less, since Toby does find ease and contentment in his miniature bowling green world. Walter, on the other hand, is constantly exacerbated by his inability to control the accidents of everyday existence through his carefully contemplated hypotheses. Toby is willing to let others do his living for him; he is content to beget children by proxy through Walter, even though he recognizes that his brother participates in these family rituals out of principle rather than for pleasure. This aspect of life Walter has succeeded in reducing to order and regularity, comparable to, and indissolubly associated with, the monthly winding of the clock. He has mortified this demand of the flesh, but in so doing has rendered himself in turn a comic character, a scapegoat. In the clash between the brothers in this episode, we have a good indication of the efficacy of each of their comic attempts to come to terms with life. Toby, by the sweetness of his nature, represents the soothing effects of cultivating one's garden (or rather bowling green), of retreating from the world and its concerns. Walter, by his irascibility, shows the results of attempting to manipulate the world, to reshape its apparent unreasonableness. Neither succeeds in living up to man's full potentiality, and their idiosyncrasies are accordingly comic. Both can succeed only by anaesthetizing parts of themselves, by refusing in their varying ways to accept the full consequences of the human state. There is, then, behind each of their deviations, an implied norm, not an ideal.

Dr. Slop, the "well-adjusted" voice of masculine wit in this scene, comes off no better than the others. He plays the part which society has taught him to think of as the appropriate one, and in so doing provides an interesting sidelight on the role of Tristram, the narrator, who is also very much alive to the merest shadow of indelicate *double entendre.* Slop is by no means as self-conscious as Tristram. He is constantly revealing his male vanity and pomposity (the pomposity which renders his fall in the mud funny rather than pathetic); he insists on his title of *accoucheur*, he cannot "bear to be out-gone," even by the learned Peireskius who walked five hundred miles to see Stevinus's renowned chariot, as against Slop's "two long miles" (though even two miles must have been quite an undertaking for the portly obstetrician). He is also a comic version of a papist, and this aspect of his character is the one exploited with the introduction of the sermon on a good conscience which inadvertently falls out of Toby's copy of the writings of Stevinus.

IV

With the finding of the sermon, Corporal Trim comes forward to occupy a central position, becoming in his turn a mask for Tristram. His naïveté is akin to that of his master, Toby, but also, like his master's brother, Walter, he seems instinctively aware of the arts of oratory, though he has received no formal training in them. In his reading of the sermon he provides indirect commentary on both brothers, as well as on

Dr. Slop. Trim is a puppet, moved by unseen strings, reading, with all the arts of elocution, words he does not fully comprehend. In this he provides an analogue of the ways in which the brothers mechanically follow their particular patterns of conduct, unaware of the larger meanings of their actions. Tristram the narrator however *is* aware, and artfully manipulates his puppets to demonstrate their inadequacies—all the while ostentatiously displaying his own "deficiencies" as a constructor of the "well-made" novel.

The sermon is the major contribution of Yorick, who was introduced so sympathetically some pages earlier. It is also the most nearly straightforward intervention of author Sterne in the entire book, though one should note that this is Sterne in his role as preacher. The sermon is a rather daring piece of foolery with sacred matters, particularly on the part of a clergyman author (as some of Sterne's readers were to complain when they learned his identity). How seriously should we take it? Sterne's motives for including it may have been mixed. Perhaps he was merely interested in puffing the two volumes of sermons he was already planning to publish. Perhaps he was seeking to indicate that Tristram's life and opinions must be read in the light of Christian doctrine as expounded by his creator. What concerns us mainly at this point, however, is its function as an element in Sterne's comic art. And the sermon is artfully introduced, thrust into the hobby-horsical conversation among the brothers Shandy and Dr. Slop. While the sermon is being read, they contrive to ride their pet horses, and Trim, the reader of the sermon, adds to the general babel by introducing a nag of his own, his understandable concern for the fate of his brother who has been taken into custody by the Inquisition. The chief device with which Sterne maintains the comic tone is this channelling of the sermon through Trim, together with the frequent interruptions by the listeners as they react in their various ways. But Sterne is not laughing *at* the sermon, though he is critically aware of the difficulties of communicating its message. This, after all, is a sermon he had preached in the cathedral of York and which he had previously published.[7] Attributed to Yorick, it seems to represent the closest thing to a straightforward "norm" against which to gauge the comedy of the first two volumes. And it is strategically placed close to the end of volume two, a position of emphasis in the original separate appearance of this segment of *Tristram Shandy*. Its serious tone is emphasized both by the levity of some of the interruptions and by the juxtaposed account of Father Shandy's obstetrical theories which occupies the closing pages of this volume.

Certainly, the meaning of this sermon as originally preached in York Minster is rather different from its meaning in the context of *Tristram Shandy*. Presumably, in both instances, it is intended to catch the conscience of its audience, but like the play within the play, this sermon within the work of comic fiction must justify itself in terms of its relevance for that audience, both the fictional one and the actual one. The reader, coming upon the sermon as just one more in a whole series of digressions, is not inclined to take it very seriously. He is first of all alerted to try to read between the lines to ascertain whether or not the composer of the sermon is a member of Dr. Slop's church (very much in the way that he had been teased previously for not grasping the clue to Mrs. Shandy's religious affiliation). The reader, like the original hearers of the sermon, is being asked to examine the state of his conscience and to ascertain its validity as a judge of his conduct. "If a man thinks at all," says the sermon, ". . . he must be privy to his own thoughts and desires." One

[7]The fullest treatment of the sermon is that of Arthur H. Cash in "The Sermon in *Tristram Shandy*," *ELH*, XXI (1964), 395–417. He finds in it "a consistent moral philosophy" strongly influenced by Locke's *Essay Concerning Human Understanding*. In this article and in *Sterne's Comedy of Moral Sentiments* (Pittsburgh, 1966), Cash gives a good account of the relations of Sterne's moral thought to the ethical theories of his time.

of the main themes of the comedy thus far has been man's unawareness of his "thoughts and desires," his tendency to function robot-like within certain stereotyped patterns. Given the stimulus, the response of Walter or Toby or Dr. Slop is eminently predictable. Much of Sterne's humour consists of exploitation of the stock response in his characters and his readers. The "norm" implied by such comedy is the very awareness of one's "own thoughts and desires" that the sermon in its initial stages takes for granted.

But this beginning is only a rhetorical trap (to which Dr. Slop, for one, falls victim). Almost immediately man's predisposition to blind himself to "the true springs and motives, which, in general, have governed the actions of his life" is pointed out in some detail, and we are forcibly reminded of such inherent human tendencies as self-love and the various passions which tend to cloud one's inner view. A quiet conscience, then, is by no means always a guiltless one, and we are provided with a series of examples to illustrate this truism. The reliability of conscience as a guide having been called in question, we are then directed to "call in religion and morality"; to see "what is written in the law of God"; to "Consult calm reason and the unchangeable obligations of justice and truth." Nevertheless, it is the individual conscience which is to "determine the matter upon these reports," not "seven watch-men that sit above upon a tower on high." The sermon goes on to argue the inseparability of religion and morality and this leads to an attack on the "Romish church," and particularly the Inquisition. The latter attack is lent some poignancy by Trim's personal involvement through his brother, and by his insistence on applying the sermon's rhetorical dramatization of the plight of the victims of the Inquisition to his brother's case, despite Walter's assurance that "this is not a history,—'tis a sermon thou art reading."

The reader has been duly warned, then, that this is a book in which a sermon by a Protestant divine can appear with the tacit approval of the author. The "norm" of this comic world, according to which its various denizens (including the narrator Tristram, though not presumably Parson Yorick, the author of the sermon) are tried and found comically wanting, is a world in which "God and reason made the law, and . . . placed conscience within you to determine . . . like a *British* judge in this land of liberty and good sense, who makes no new law, but faithfully declares that law which he knows already written."

Narrator Tristram almost immediately reveals his own rather mercenary reason for including the sermon by informing the public that it is only a sample of Yorick's powers, and that enough more of his sermons are available to make a handsome volume. Thus sermons become commodities. The jester intends that the world should pay in cash for any spiritual benefits to be obtained from them. The few remaining pages of volume two are taken up with a further account of Walter Shandy's eccentricities, especially his obsession with the notion that all humans are in jeopardy at the crucial moment of birth, and that in most cases the head of the infant is inevitably damaged by the pressures brought to bear upon it as it is thrust into the world, unless it is fortunate enough to be delivered feet first or by Caesarean section. The implication is that man knows better than God in matters of childbirth (the whole theory has Freudian overtones). In any event, Walter's pride in this theory, as usual, goes before a fall. His comic flaw is his constant concern "that so many things in this world were out of joint" and his naïve belief that he had been born to set them right. Thus he "would see nothing in the light in which others placed it . . . would weigh nothing in common scales."

He is certainly not inclined to follow the dictates of the sermon, to which he listened with such apparent approval, to make no new law, but faithfully to declare that law which he knows already written. He claims that he has no wish to tamper with the "foundations of our excellent constitution in church and state" and that his principal object of attack is "minute error" which creeps in through the "small crevices, which human nature leaves unguarded" and undermines the entire structure. In fact, the theories and hypotheses with which he seeks to eliminate such error are themselves somewhat unsettling. Taking as his point of departure in this instance the contention that all souls are equal before God, he then goes on to consider the inexplicable inequalities that obviously exist among men. How to explain the fact that some men are much more gifted than others, how to account for the genius in particular—this is his chief concern, especially since he considers himself to have a touch of genius and would certainly like his child to have outstanding mental qualities. He accepts the traditional relationship between the soul and the human mind and sets himself to elaborate on the Cartesian body-soul dualism. It seems obvious to him that, despite the importance of due care in the act of propagation and in choosing a name for the child, the most significant concern of all is "the preservation of this delicate and fine-spun web" which constitutes the centre of mental powers. This then is Walter's scheme for the salvation of man's soul: reverse the usual order of childbirth, allow the infant to make its entrance feet first rather than head first, and thus minimize the pressures on the tender young cranium and the consequent danger of damage to the brain, which Walter firmly associates with the soul. He has no apparent concern with moral conduct as a revelation of the quality of soul, the main subject of the sermon so artfully juxtaposed with Walter's theory.

Volume two ends with the clown-narrator daring his readers to guess what they will find in subsequent instalments and giving them some hints to pique their curiosity. This is a comic version of the inevitable "continued in our next" technique almost forced on authors of works published in parts. Tristram uses this hoary device as part of the comic pattern of his gradually accumulating volumes. They can appear only at intervals, since he must be allowed time for their composition, and paradoxically, the longer it takes him to write them, the greater is the backlog of material waiting to be related. Here is one more analogue of the frustrations attendant upon participating in the human condition. And, in laughing at Tristram's often ludicrous efforts to tell all, presumably so that his audience will understand and forgive his present clownish condition, the reader sees in comic perspective his own constant (and usually futile) efforts at self-justification, his own tendency to blame the small accidents of fate for his shortcomings, his own failure to look squarely and conscientiously at his own moral responsibilities and to undertake the sort of self-scrutiny which forms the basis of a valid "good conscience" as described in Yorick's sermon. Like the laughter aroused by all great clowns, a good deal of Tristram's humour stems from recognition of ludicrous aspects of oneself in the antics of the clown figure. This is sympathetic laughter, rather than derisive. Comedy tends to present a glass in which we glimpse ourselves (albeit distorted for humorous effect), whereas satire, as Swift wryly put it, presents a glass in which we tend to see others' failings, but seldom, willingly, our own.

VOLUMES THREE AND FOUR

Although *Tristram Shandy* was published in instalments, it contains, as commentators have noted, various over-all, in a sense, unifying patterns. Nevertheless, it was brought into being in segments and their original separate publication gives them a measure of individual autonomy. The first two volumes serve to introduce the main cast of characters (only the Widow Wadman among the principals does not make a personal appearance), and especially to establish the relationship between narrator Tristram and the reader. How we react to Tristram determines our attitude to the entire novel. He thus figures prominently in these early volumes. Walter and Toby enter, are described, and perform, but it is Tristram's interchanges with the reader that take up the bulk of the space. This is as it should be in a fictional world dominated by the cap and bells.

The digressive style of *Tristram Shandy* makes the transition from volume to volume only a particular instance of the many transitions which are such a feature of the book's narrative structure. Volume three opens with the repetition of Uncle Toby's unsettling interruption of Dr. Slop's account of the marvels wrought by improvements in the science of obstetrics (his naïvely witty remark about the prodigious armies that had been born to fight in Flanders without benefit of Dr. Slop's obstetrical knowledge), an interruption which had itself been left hanging unanswered while Tristram expounded Father Shandy's theories about childbirth. Toby's remark is equally relevant as a commentary on Walter's proposals, since, as Tristram points out, Father Shandy and Dr. Slop are in firm coalition in matters obstetrical. The reader is directed by a footnote to refresh his mind on these things as he recommences consideration of them at the start of volume three. (One must bear in mind, too, that between the publication of the first two volumes and the second two had come the first selection of *Sermons by Mr. Yorick.*. Sterne could now count on his readers to think of him as a clergyman, to some extent equivalent to Yorick, and thus not to identify him with Tristram, or only in so far as he could be imagined as deliberately donning cap and bells for the performance. He might also not unreasonably expect his readers to be aware of some of the main themes in his published sermons and of the ways in which they echoed and reinforced the sermon in volume two.)[8]

But consideration of Toby's remark is still further delayed

[8]See discussion in chap. vi.

at this point by some typically Shandean buffoonery. Tristram shows how Slop should have parried Toby's innocently shrewd thrust, but instead Slop is reduced to "perplexed vacuity of eye." And when Father Shandy attempts to rescue the discussion he, too, is involved in the clownish confusion of attempting to retrieve his handkerchief from his right coat pocket while his right hand is engaged in holding on to his wig, a feat rendered ludicrously difficult by the fact that the fashion of the moment decreed that coat pockets should be cut low down in the skirt. All of this is leading up to chapter four in which Tristram talks of "Messrs. the monthly Reviewers" and their treatment of the first two volumes of Yorick's *Sermons*. They have ruffled his jerkin, very much in the manner that Father Shandy has twisted his coat by the "transverse zig-zaggery" of his approach. As author, he claims to be stoically untouched by their comments, certainly not ruffled in the way that Father Shandy is by his self-imposed frustrations. But Tristram's frustrations, too, are in a sense self-imposed; by appearing as author, by attempting to communicate, he invited misunderstanding, lack of comprehension, particularly in choosing to make his appearance in the guise of clown and in following this performance so closely with a change into clerical garb. The readers might be excused for confusing the two roles, or for asking questions about the "essential" person lurking behind these public personae.

I

As has been indicated, *Tristram Shandy* continues the tradition established by Erasmus' *Praise of Folly*.[9] Tristram is to some extent the "wise fool," but he also shares the split personality of others in this tradition: Rabelais' Panurge and Pantagruel, Cervantes' Don Quixote and Sancho Panza. Sterne's comic irony is, then, in a measure Erasmian, though

[9] See Traugott, *Tristram Shandy's World*, pp. 39 and 138–39.

it has undergone many changes from the original. The main difficulty with Erasmian irony (as a recent commentator points out)[10] is in trying to assess its complex significance. It cannot simply be turned upside down—both of its polar meanings must be given full consideration. The implications of Sterne's irony, like Erasmus', are not quite so obvious as some readers have assumed. Most of the characters in *Tristram Shandy* are "fools," though they represent different kinds of folly. In the discussion among the characters (and between Tristram and his critics) which takes place in the early stages of volume three, there is a good demonstration of this aspect of Sterne's ironic art. Dr. Slop and Walter Shandy are both revealed in all their inhumane narrowness by Toby's simple assertion: "I wish you had seen what prodigious armies we had in Flanders." Dr. Slop is left speechless, unable to grasp the fact that a good many babies have been born without the benefit of the obstetrical innovations in which he takes such inordinate professional pride. Walter, too, finds it difficult to fend off Toby's innocent yet devastating queries about the actual worth of his own theories which he considers so potentially revolutionary in their implications. Toby's naïveté is at the same time exposed by the example he chooses. He seems blind to the implicit irony of connecting efforts to improve methods of childbirth with the still more prodigious armies bent on the mutual destruction which will be the inevitable result of the success of such efforts.

Meanwhile, Tristram as narrator is mainly concerned with demonstrating Toby's benevolence, his tolerance of all living creatures, including flies, as a paradigm for his own tolerance, as author, of the critics who buzz about his ears. Toby, then, like the traditional "wise" fool, is on the side of nature against human attempts to institutionalize man's instincts, to produce various barren versions of Utopia by eliminating the unpredictable. However, ironically, his own actions are eminently

[10]Walter Kaiser, *Praisers of Folly* (Cambridge, Mass., 1963), pp. 92–93.

predictable—his own human passions, extravagantly mild. Tristram, too, a version of the "wise fool," denounces rules because they falsify reality, but, paradoxically, as author, he creates order in the very act of simulating disorder, and follows established traditions at the very time he is boasting of his uniqueness. And, again paradoxically, he makes such individual use of traditional materials that he produces a work which is in fact *sui generis*.

In essence, Tristram's narrative is an account of the numerous "small accidents" which have produced him, and hence his book. The anecdote of Obadiah and Dr. Slop's "green bays bag" which follows at this point is typical. Obadiah and Dr. Slop's maid do what seems quite sensible in binding the bag securely so that none of the obstetrical instruments which it contains will bounce out as Obadiah gallops back to Shandy Hall. But unfortunately they still jingle inside the bag, and Obadiah is led to tie them even more securely with the hatband. The resulting difficulties which Dr. Slop has in untying the knots (which in turn delay him in proceeding to aid the midwife in the delivery of Tristram) are obviously emblematic of the narrator Tristram's constantly frustrated efforts to deliver himself of his book. Millions of thoughts swim daily in "the thin juice" of his understanding, and their constant collisions and coruscations are vividly reflected in the topsy-turvy patterns of his book. For the time being, Dr. Slop is the buffoon in the centre of the stage, clownishly struggling with the "devilish tight, hard knots," meanwhile cursing Obadiah in a rising crescendo which reaches its peak as he inadvertently slashes his thumb in attempting to cut the cords. At this juncture, Walter supplies him with a pre-fabricated curse, that of Ernulphus.

The humour of the situation lies partly in the pronouncement of such thorough damnation for such a trivial offence, partly in having the papist Slop self-consciously deliver the curse to the accompaniment of Uncle Toby's whistling. We are obviously meant to relate this occasion to the one shortly previous in which Trim read the sermon to the accompaniment of Dr. Slop's comments. The sermon contained a dramatic attack on the Church of Rome, in particular on its cruelty to those outside its beliefs. This cursing of Obadiah is presumably just another example of Romish intolerance. However, no one seems to take the curse very seriously, not even Dr. Slop. It accomplishes for him what Walter suggested it might—it gives vent to his feelings. Tristram, like his father, is interested in it mainly as a curiosity, as well as a comic device. He inserts his irreverent oath by the beards of the "heathen worships" to reinforce his wish that he could have been present to observe the scene in person, and he seems to side with Uncle Toby in his assertion that he would not curse the devil himself with so much bitterness. However, Dr. Slop quickly points out that the devil is, by definition, "cursed, and damn'd already, to all eternity." Here again, as in the sermon, we have solemn matters made the occasion of jest. Tristram immediately delivers a mock-encomium on the curse, claiming (along with his father though with slightly different supporting arguments) that all subsequent curses are merely pale imitations of it. In the process, he takes the opportunity to castigate once more the critics who insist on judging dogmatically by pedantic rules. He treats the curse, then, as a piece of rhetoric, demonstrating the gusto of its originator. His attitude to it is rather like that of members of the Hell-Fire Club (or its branch at Hall-Stevenson's Crazy Castle to which Sterne is said to have belonged).

Volumes three and four are noticeably more eccentric than volumes one and two. The digressions are more abrupt, their comic relevance not so apparent and, at times, Tristram seems to be almost parodying his own Shandy-manner. The thread of narrative in volume three is slight; the "action" is focused in the wings while the major event, the birth of Tristram, takes place on a stage whose curtains are drawn. All we hear

are various noises "off," and the fragmentary reports of mes-
sengers. And, throughout, Tristram constantly intervenes with
his mock-erudite explorations of a whole series of by-paths.
If we were reading for story, all this would be infuriating.
Clearly Sterne is seeking to entertain us in other ways. In this
comic world conjured up by Tristram we are bombarded with
incongruities, with seeming absurdities—he is forever playing
jokes on his characters, on his audience, and (in true clown
fashion) on himself, because the less successful his efforts to
get his story told, the more incompetent does he appear as
story-teller. He keeps excusing himself on various grounds:
the misfortunes that attended his birth and upbringing, the
intractableness of his material, the impossibility, for the curious
mind, of resisting any aspect of truth.

"Truth"—whole and nothing but—then, is his ostensible
subject. And most of his cast of characters, too, share a like
obsession. Dr. Slop is fascinated by the various possibilities
involved in the delivery of a child, as is Walter Shandy, but
with rather different emphases. Toby, on the other hand, is
concerned mainly with the safety of mother and child, until,
that is, he is distracted by some slanting reference to his own
particular domain of knowledge, the science of fortification.
Tristram, meanwhile, keeps us aware of the fact that *he* is the
child about to be born who is being so variously regarded by
these three. The comic irony is elaborate yet simple. A com-
plicating factor, however, is Tristram's own inability to fix his
mind on his narrative for very long at a stretch, his obsessive
concern with the machinery of communication, a concern
which, paradoxically, consistently gets in the way of what he
is presumbaly trying to communicate. Tristram's characters
are also frequently sidetracked into discussions of all manner
of seeming irrelevancies. At this particular juncture, for
instance, Walter and Toby engage in a fruitless discussion of
Locke's theories of duration and its simple modes. This, of
course, is a burlesque of Locke, and raises problems similar to

those we have previously noted concerning the jocular treatment of basically serious matters. One can hardly expect a
clown to be taken seriously as a philosopher, yet he may utter,
in his simplicity, some profound observations without really
understanding what he has said. In this very discussion, Toby,
in true comic fashion, cuts the ground from underneath
Walter's loaded observation about the way in which two hours
can sometimes seem an age—intended as an opening gambit
for a demonstration of his own grasp of the epistemological
problems involved—by giving him pat the Lockean solution
that it was due to "the succession of our ideas." Walter naturally does a double-take. But he is soon able to reveal that Toby
is merely parroting words which for him have no meaning.
(Quite possibly he has heard Walter expound on this subject
before.) Walter then, not easily put off, proceeds to give his
paraphrase of Locke on this subject, ostensibly to exchange
Toby's "honest ignorance" for knowledge. He succeeds only
in puzzling him to death and, eventually, putting them both
to sleep. Sterne presumably expects his readers to be familiar
enough with Locke to laugh at Walter's difficulties in explaining him to Toby. Are they also meant to laugh at Locke? To
what extent is he to be taken as seriously as the Gospel is in
the sermon on the good conscience? Both Locke and the
sermon are presented to us in a context which demands that
we look at them critically, that we examine the way in which
they are able to stand up to the test of ridicule. The name of
Locke is here coupled with that of Lucian and Rabelais and
Cervantes, and all four are associated with discourses upon
TIME and ETERNITY. But the whole investigation dissipates
in clouds and thick darkness as the two participants nod off
before the fire.

II

At this point Tristram inserts his "Author's Preface," casting
himself as usual in the part of the "wise fool," and adopting

for the purpose a mask reminiscent of Rabelais'. His announced theme is the nature of wit and judgment, their compatability or otherwise, and he takes as his text Locke's assertions about the differences between the two. The style echoes that of Swift's *Tale of a Tub*, inasmuch as both are to an extent parodies of hack writing. Tristram pursues with mock seriousness the implications of some of the conventional prefatory comments, such as the wish that his book may be blessed with readers possessing *both* wit and judgment. If all mankind were witty and wise obviously his book would never have come into being. On the other hand, how is one to account for the manifestly inequitable distribution of these desirable qualities among the human species (a question that he has raised previously in his book)? Environment is assuredly a factor; the demands of different climates may, for example, be a decisive catalyst. But the conclusion Tristram is moving towards is the not very startling one that "of these two luminaries," wit and judgment, "so much of their irradiations are suffered from time to time to shine down upon us; as he, whose infinite wisdom which dispenses every thing in exact weight and measure, knows will just serve to light us on our way in this night of our obscurity" (III, xx, 198). We are now very close to the matter and the manner characteristic of Yorick, and in fact the preface is rather like one of his sermons, livened up a bit to make it suitable to Tristram. We are given, as we often are in the sermons, a series of graphic illustrations of the shortcomings of the world, on this occasion those stemming from lack of intelligence, from lack of wit and judgment. This leads Tristram, naturally, to a defence of men of wit as being more wisely judicious than those "great wigs" or "long beards" who by their gravity (in all its senses) have imposed themselves on the world (and on John Locke) as men of judgment. And he illustrates his argument with the witty comparison of wit and judgment to the two knobs on the back of a chair—one without the other makes the whole lack symmetry and balance. He has admitted freely early in the preface that an illustration is not an argument; nevertheless, it serves "to clarify the understanding, previous to the application of the argument itself." And the "application" here is an attack on "grave folks" (particularly, it is implied, grave critics) who set themselves up as wise judges competent to heap contempt upon "injudicious" wits. "I write not for them," proclaims Tristram, ending his misplaced preface with a flourish.

This then is a statement from Tristram comparable to that of Yorick in his inserted sermon. True, Tristram is constantly thrusting himself forward to address the reader, but this particular intrusion is deliberately marked off from the others, and, despite its Shandean tone, its argument is set forth in a more systematic manner and it is longer than the other digressions. On the other hand, it is not placed in the context of a group of critical commentators as are the sermon and the Curse of Ernulphus. Are we then to take it seriously as an attack on one of Locke's propositions?[11] This is, after all, a mock preface, a display of ingenuity. We are meant to be aware of the ironies involved in the witty defence of wit by a wit. It is plainly not intended to convince the "grave" members of the audience. Its analogy between wit and judgment and the knobs on a chair is a clever parody of the tendency of philosophers to use common objects about them, particularly furniture, to illustrate their propositions. The "argument" proves nothing, but it exhibits the author's wit. As to his "judgment," too large an infusion of that would surely ruin the narrator's role as clown. The judgment may well be implicit, but if it becomes explicit gaiety disappears. Wit must outbalance sober judgment in the world of comedy. Like Walter Shandy's, Tristram's "rhetoric and conduct" are, in the preface, "at perpetual handy-cuffs." But this after all is only another way of noting that he is playing the role of the

[11]See Traugott's discussion in *Tristram Shandy's World*, pp. 65–73.

"wise fool" whose foolish conduct, designed to amuse, is also designed to demonstrate the foolishness of the world which laughs at him in part because it recognizes a comically distorted image of itself.

In the chapter following the preface, Walter Shandy is castigated (and through him men in general) for inability to put reason, and the knowledge resulting from its application, to practical use; man's tendency to "struggle against evils which cannot be avoided, and submit to others, which a tenth part of the trouble they create him, would remove from his heart for ever" (III, xxi, 203). For example, the creak of the unoiled hinges on the parlour-door when it is pushed open by Corporal Trim awakens the sleeping Walter and Toby. But for the noisy hinges, Trim would have slipped away without disturbing the brothers in their after-dinner nap, and the ensuing conversation would not have taken place.

This chain of events, again, is typical of the narrative as a whole as it is projected by Tristram. Tristram, himself, the narrator, would not be as he is except for a series of "small accidents." Each of these "accidents," in turn, as they are presented by him, comes into being through still other fortuitous circumstances, circumstances, which, in their turn, depend for their effect, and sometimes (as with the faulty hinges) for their very being, on the existence of characters such as Walter and Toby and the others. The apparently random structure of the book thus provides a comical commentary on absurd chains of cause and effect so often evident in human experience. And yet, ironically, the randomness is only apparent. Tristram, as narrator, while denying that he follows any man's rules, in fact follows certain patterns which soon become fairly familiar to the reader. For instance, one does not have to read very far before the reactions of Toby to any mention of forts or sieges become predictable. Walter's bent for theorizing, and his favourite theories, become easily recognizable elements in the game Tristram plays with his audience. The elements of Tristram's own style as narrator, the inevitability of his digressions (though not their content), his comments on the frustrations experienced by the writer are definite parts of the "logic" guiding this world, a logic rather easier to understand than that governing the real world, but in its way a comic representation of that world. If the reader is willing to follow the "rules," to participate in the labyrinthine design of the game, he experiences the delights of the world of play.[12]

As another structural pattern, time in *Tristram Shandy* is a continuous present. The focus is on the act of creation, though the "events" recorded all have their being in the past.[13] The structure is a mosaic, depending for its continuity on an alignment between reader and author. The various pieces of narrative are constantly interrupted by the author's intrusive comments, but these comments, which function as a sort of refrain (or as a mock version of the Chorus in classical Greek drama), are, paradoxically, the binding element in the composition. Their recurrence keeps us aware of Tristram, the

[12]The spirit of play permeates *Tristram Shandy*. Tristram plays at recording his life and opinions, toying with the reader throughout, casting both himself and his reader in roles to fit the occasion. Toby plays at battles on the bowling green, and tries, Quixote-like, to play at the game of love with the Widow Wadman—with disturbing results when reality breaks in. Walter plays with his theories and also becomes ludicrous, and, like Toby, a trifle pathetic, when he tries to apply them to life. The clash between play and non-play provides a good many of the tensions which add serious tones to the comic game. Ever and anon Tristram himself is awakened to harsh facts of life by reminders of the inevitable end of the game—death. But he then plays harder than ever; life is bearable only if he treats it as a game. The reader is involved in the very process of the production of the book. He is in a sense a co-author and co-player in the game.
Of course, as J. Huizanga points out, "The comic comes under the category of non-seriousness. . . . But its relation to play is subsidiary. In itself play is not comical either for player or public. . . . The mimic and laughter-provoking art of the clown is comic as well as ludicrous, but it can scarcely be termed genuine play"; *Homo Ludens* (Boston, 1955), p. 6.
[13]See Northrop Frye, "Towards Defining an Age of Sensibility," *ELH*, XXIII (1956), 145: ". . . the sense of literature as process was brought to a peculiarly exquisite perfection by Sterne. . . ."

narrator, and forces us to meditate with him on the difficulties of narration and the significance, if any, of the various anecdotes he has set out to relate. But Tristram is not the artist as bard or oracle.[14] His attitude is ironic. His allusions are mainly parodic. The medium for his imagination is prose. But one must bear in mind that his is the prose of a preacher, if not of a prophet.

Tristram, however, despite references to his two bad cassocks, is a most unparsonlike preacher. As clown, he is fascinated by the passionate forces in humans which, by getting astride of vaunted reason, render men ludicrous. And the sexual passion is the one which lends itself most readily to comic use. (Aggressive instincts are another comic staple. The Curse of Ernulphus is an excellent example of man as anathematizer reduced to comic proportions.) Since Tristram's stage is the printed page, his humour is verbal humour, and play on words is one of his favourite devices, particularly the manipulation of suggestive euphemisms. This verbal play is very prominent in volumes three and four, especially with reference to the word "nose" and its implications. Midway through volume three we are alerted to the confusion between head and hip which, in the delivery of an infant, can mean the difference between Dr. Slop's forceps crushing his nose or his genitals. Walter Shandy is naturally horrified at the latter possibility, but is, as it turns out, just as perturbed when the former takes place. Meanwhile, the gap between these two aspects of the body is further narrowed by the anecdote of Trim and Bridget and the mysterious destruction, one moonlit night, of Uncle Toby's curious draw-bridge as these two were strolling across it. Subsequent references to "bridge" inevitably suggest to Toby the new one that Trim is fabricating to take the place of the one demolished. But the bridge

---

[14]He is not a Blake or a Christopher Smart, though parts of the *Jubilate Agno* have a Shandean quality, and Blake's *An Island in the Moon* is in the Sterne tradition.

which Trim is in fact reporting on after his entrance awakens the sleeping brothers is the one being prepared by Dr. Slop to replace the crushed bridge of the new-born Tristram's nose. This leads full force into the topic of noses and Walter Shandy's obsession with them. With mock precision Tristram declares that by the word *Nose* he means "a Nose, and nothing more, or less." With mock gravity he describes his book as one "of strict morality and close reasoning," and yet one in which, because of the equivocal nature of language, he is unfortunately dependent on the cleanliness of his reader's imagination.[15]

The "world" which Tristram projects is a verbal universe in which the words themselves, the building blocks, are of uncertain and shifting status. A good deal of the word-play in these volumes is bawdy; Tristram rings the changes on sexual euphemisms, inveigling the reader into hyper-awareness of possible double meanings in the most innocent seeming terms. The "nosology" which bulks so large in these chapters is Tristram's development of the tradition of phallic by-play associated with the antics of the clown from the earliest times. Though Walter is the immediate cause of laughter in the description of his fanatical interest in noses and their relation to male potency, Tristram, as in most of the jokes in the book, is the ultimate butt. It is Tristram whose nose is crushed, Tristram who is misnamed, Tristram who not only falls heir to the misfortunes which his father seeks so ineptly to avoid but also inherits from his father the very eccentricities which have resulted in his inauspicious birth and breeding. Slawken-bergius' fable of the stranger with the long nose derives a

---

[15]References to Rabelais seem more numerous in these chapters. A number of them are to Book IV of *Gargantua and Pantagruel*, and the Erasmus of *Colloquia Familiaria* also makes an appearance. Certainly, Tristram seems here to be modelling his narrative on Rabelais more obviously than heretofore. On the other hand, Hafen Slawkenbergius, the renowned authority on the subject of noses so revered by Walter Shandy, is described in terms not inapplicable to Burton and his absorption in the subject of melancholy.

good deal of its humour from the fact that it is being related by short-nosed Tristram.

III

Slawkenbergius's Tale comes at the beginning of volume four and thus occupies a central position in this instalment of *Tristram Shandy*, comparable to that of the sermon's climactic place at the end of the first two volumes. The Tale, making up as it does better than a quarter of volume four, is considerably longer than the sermon, even if one includes the commentary on the latter. The Tale is interrupted only briefly by remarks of Walter and Toby, and these remarks belong to previous readings, not to the occasion of Tristram's present translation. It is an inserted story after the fashion of Fielding and Cervantes, but in manner reminiscent of Rabelais, representing a clowning version of the quest for truth rather like that of Panurge in Book Three of *Gargantua and Pantagruel*.[16] The "truth" about marriage is what Panurge seeks; the "truth" about the stranger's nose is the focal point for Slawkenbergius. Just as Rabelais has Panurge pursue his quest in various directions, seeking help from numerous sources, so does the stranger's nose foment discussions of different kinds among different groups. The stranger himself turns out to be a lover fleeing from the doubts of his loved one—doubts, of course, concerning his nose. Entering the town of Strasburg on his way to Frankfort, he raises a storm of controversy. All those who see him have an overpowering urge to touch the stranger's nose in order to test its reality. But the stranger refuses to be touched, and goes his way astride his mule, leaving behind him an uproar about his nose.

The common folk—the bandy-legged drummer, the trumpeter and his wife, the inn-keeper and his wife—take a direct

---

[16]See Kaiser, *Praisers of Folly*, p. 125: "The subject of the *Tiers Livre* is truth and not, as has so generally been said, marriage. Panurge the fool is not seeking a wife; he is seeking an answer."

approach: if the nose can be touched and felt, if it bleeds, if it has a pimple on it, it is real. All those who have actually seen the nose are soon giving lectures upon it to the "un-learned" who, like themselves, are anxious for "facts." But meanwhile the "learned" members of the community are busy approaching truth by a different route, "pumping her up thro' the conduits of dialect [sic] induction—they concerned themselves not with facts—they reasoned—" (IV, 257). The medical faculty, the logicians, the lawyers, the two universities of Strasburg—the Lutheran and the Popish—all join in the fray.

Meanwhile, the stranger is overtaken by the brother of his loved one, Julia, and on reading a letter from her, returns to her directly with overflowing heart, by-passing Strasburg, whose citizens have been rendered so vulnerable by their curiosity, by their search for the truth about the stranger's nose, that they forget all about practical matters of self-defence and are easily conquered by the French. Truth obviously is elusive, and human interest in it is variously motivated: some-times mere curiosity provides the spur, but just as often some form of self-interest is involved. The ambiguities in the mean-ing of "nose" played upon by Tristram also play upon the imaginations of the Strasburgers in determining their different involvements in the pursuit of truth in nasal form.

Does Slawkenbergius's Tale function as a "norm" in any-thing like the manner of the sermon on a good conscience? Inasmuch as it is fable or allegory it does provide critical commentary on Tristram Shandy's fictional world. It is not a more or less direct statement of a position, as is the sermon, but it is a story told by a clown, albeit a "wise" clown. The Strasburgers are comparable to Tristram's readers in their curiosity, their easily heated imaginations, their lust for truth, and the ease with which they are led astray in their search for it. Tristram, in his Slawkenbergian mask, guys them. To the Strasburgers, the stranger is a phenomenon rather than a person. Their various interests in his nose are ultimately motivated by self-interest. They are totally unaware of him as unhappy lover, fleeing from disappointment. To his critics, Tristram, too, is mainly freak rather than flesh and blood. From time to time, in his references to Jenny for example, he tries to insinuate that he, like the stranger, might be viewed as romantic lover. But, of course, as clown, he cannot expect to be taken seriously in this role. The stranger was given his identity, his part to play, by the gods at the "promontory of noses." Tristram was also created clown by the *mélange* of circumstances which he details in his book. Such parallels as these between the Tale and Tristram's story are inexact, but suggestive. But in their search for the "truth" of this small segment, Tristram's readers might well become more aware of the ironic implications of the work as a whole.

The ostensible reason for Tristram's inserting a sample of Slawkenbergius' story-telling (and offering to supply further examples if there is any demand for them, just as he had done with Yorick's sample sermon) is to provide a background on Walter Shandy's fanatical concern with the subject of noses so that we can better appreciate his reactions to the news of the mishap to his son's nose. But the "lashes" he suffers at this latest accident are immediately put into an ironical perspective by Toby's predictable reaction: he is at once reminded of the unmerciful whipping of a grenadier at Bruges. And Trim's reaction to this memory and the accompanying recollections of his brother Tom's plight ("these are misfortunes, may it please your honour, worth lying down and crying over") bring a blush to the face of the recumbent Walter Shandy.

Understandably, Walter is led to speculate on the vicissitudes of man's fate, and on his ability to recover from the "cross reckonings . . . with which the heart of man is overcharged." Toby suggests that "we are upheld by the grace and assistance of the best of Beings" (echoing phrases that might easily find their place in one of Yorick's sermons). But Walter brushes aside talk of religion. His metaphor is mechanical, not spiritual: man, the well-ordered machine, has a built-in spring which counterbalances the shock of evil. Since the greatest evil has befallen his new-born son, he must counteract it with the greatest good by giving him the greatest name: Trismegistus. Certainly Walter Shandy's world does not operate like a well-ordered machine, even though Walter himself as presented by Tristram has many robot-like characteristics. Whatever plan Walter decides to put into operation in connection with his son perversely brings into being the very opposite of what he intended. He is comically impotent in the face of circumstance. Try as he will to manipulate the large forces of life in the manner described in the esoteric books he is forever dipping into, he is constantly thwarted by small events, seeming inconsequentialities. But soon recovering, he makes yet another sortie against the world of chance, still desperately seeking to impose order, even if only by calculating odds, as in the "chapter of chances" (IV, ix, 279).

Walter is not the only victim of crass casualty; the other characters, too, are vulnerable. And Tristram's book is ever at the mercy of stray impulses which jar the unstable narrator off his course. In addition, it is Tristram's avowed intention to make it his rule to "do all things out of all rule." So Toby and Walter are left on the stairs while Tristram writes his chapter upon chapters and his chapter upon the difficulty of getting them off the stairs and into bed, in which he is able to elaborate on the impossibility of the task of any autobiographer who tries to tell all. The comic exaggeration underlines the problems faced by a novelist such as Richardson and humorously draws attention to the gap between life and art, in particular the art which uses as its medium the printed word.

IV

The remainder of volume four has to do with the christening of Tristram and the efforts of Walter Shandy to undo this further misadventure. The usual intrusive commentaries by Tristram are evident, including (in chapter twenty-two) his denial that his book is written against anything, except perhaps the spleen, in order "to drive the *gall* and other *bitter juices* from the gall bladder, liver and sweet-bread of his majesty's subjects, with all the inimicitious passions which belong to them, down into their duodenums." The canonical dinner and the incident of the hot chestnut are certainly calculated to exercise "the intercostal and abdominal muscles in laughter."

Yorick makes another short appearance at this juncture. He it is who advises attendance at the canonical dinner so that a full and official discussion of the possibility of undoing the christening of Tristram may be instigated. "All that is requisite," says Yorick, "is to apprize *Didius*, and let him manage a conversation after dinner so as to introduce the subject . . ." (IV, xxiii, 302). But it is Yorick himself who foments discussion by tearing the sermon he has just delivered to the group into strips for pipe lighters. This debate is abruptly deflected by the exclamation wrung from Phutatorius by the hot chestnut. Because he picks up and eats the offending chestnut when it is cast out by Phutatorius, Yorick is immediately suspected of having dropped it into the front of the victim's galligaskins, partly as a prank and partly as a witty criticism of Phutatorius' book entitled *Of Keeping Concubines*. He is in fact blameless, but Tristram makes the point that, as "a man of jest," he was automatically deemed capable of this sort of indecorous practical joking, and, because of a constitutional inability to bring himself to deny what he felt were such manifest misreadings of his character, he implicitly accepted this and other imputations "of saying and doing

a thousand things of which . . . his nature was incapable"
(IV, xxvii, 324).

Tristram is here making on behalf of Yorick the denial he
refuses to make for himself. At the same time he is echoing
his own tongue-in-cheek disavowals of bawdy intent in his
deliberate play on the meanings of words. He is setting up
Yorick as an ideal, a prototype of himself, and yet at the same
time he is judging himself, and to an extent the reader who
shares his taste for *double entendre*. Thus Tristram in his
clown role speaks truer than he realizes, and in defending
Yorick condemns himself. Behind both characters, author
Sterne is ironically aware of the implications for himself contained in the words he has Tristram utter. Wittily, he adjoins
to Tristram's words a brief chapter in which remedies for
Phutatorius' accidental burn are discussed. Eugenius pre-
scribes "a soft sheet of paper just come off the press," though
it soon is made clear that different printed sheets will have
different effects. However, the point being made is a valid
one—Tristram's clowning, bawdy or not, will hardly tend to
inflame sexual passions, even those already warmed by hot
chestnuts, but will in fact tend to have the opposite effect
of producing a comic catharsis by rousing laughter at man's
ridiculous subjection to his physical appetites.

"True Shandeism," says Tristram at the end of volume four
(337–38), "think what you will against it, opens the heart
and lungs, and like all those affections which partake of its
nature, it forces the blood and other vital fluids of the body
to run freely thro' its channels, and makes the wheel of life
run long and chearfully round." And so he takes his leave
"till this time twelve-month," unless, he adds parenthetically,
"this vile cough kills me in the mean time." This is tossed
in lightly, apparently as an afterthought, but, knowing the
facts of Sterne's physical condition, we are not deceived. The
author is intimately acquainted with the spectre of death; he
has stood on his doorstep on more than one occasion. This

knowledge adds some pathos to our reaction to Tristram's foolery. But this awareness of human mortality as the most drastic of human frailties is inherent in the clown's dramatization of man's various limitations. Tristram, as clown, stresses particularly the beginning and the end of life: the hazards attendant on arrival and departure. The journey in between is taken note of mainly in accounts of other characters. The picture we get is of a creature whose destiny is radically beyond his control. Man, at the mercy of small chances, can be viewed as absurdly comic in his self-importance. He can also be seen as pathetic in his self-awareness. Sterne's comedy is a mingling of these two attitudes, though the pathos is more evident in the later volumes of *Tristram Shandy* and in *A Sentimental Journey*.

In part, as he hints, Sterne writes his books to amuse himself as well as others, to fend off melancholy awareness by laughing at it, much as Burton in his *Anatomy* undertakes his exhaustive account of melancholy to avoid falling prey to it.[17] Tristram, as clown-artist, writes for society and yet is set apart from it by his talents. Yet society, inasmuch as it forms his audience, his reason for being, claims the right to criticize him, even though as he complains, many of its criticisms are wrong-headed because the critics, as non-artists, have failed to understand his insights. By the same token, as an artist he must have failed to communicate these insights to them. Which, then, should be castigated—his failure or theirs? At the same time, Tristram seems to cut himself off also from other artists, since he claims to be an "original," to make his own rules. This is another way of saying that he is shaping the destiny of his book, forming it out of chaos. But we are meant to laugh at these claims, because Tristram is constantly drawing attention to his debts to other authors, and gleefully uses the words of Burton to denounce those authors who

[17]Burton, incidentally, contributes significantly, though without specific acknowledgment, to volume five; see *infra*, Appendix.

borrow (V, i, 342). And the "form" which he creates is a comically chaotic one. He, like Walter, is at the mercy of small chances in his attempts to design order. We have in Tristram a comic portrait of the artist, and a comic analogue of the human predicament: man's constantly frustrated efforts to overcome the built-in limitations of his condition, efforts which could, ironically, only succeed by eliminating most of the recognizably human characteristics, and by producing a new species, far more angel-like than man.

VOLUMES FIVE TO NINE

Incongruity is one of the elements in comedy most often commented upon. Tristram is something of a specialist in incongruous juxtapositions. At the end of volume four, Walter Shandy, just returned from the canonical dinner, is plunged into fresh speculations by news of Aunt Dinah's legacy. What should he do with the thousand pounds: should he enclose the great Ox-moor, or send his son Bobby upon his travels? He is rescued from this dilemma by news of yet another misfortune: his son Bobby's death. Tristram comments: "What is the life of man! Is it not to shift from side to side?— from sorrow to sorrow?" But this death is not to be an occasion for pathos. Bobby is never more than a name in Tristram's life. His demise means only that Tristram is now heir-apparent to the Shandy family, thus adding significance to the train of misfortunes which have attended the birth of this small hero. Bobby's passing provides the occasion in the opening stages of volume five for some witty scenes devoted to self-centred reactions to the death of a fellow human being— reactions which are defensive or self-protective in nature. Tristram himself flees from the fact of death into thoughts of the busy writing career that stretches limitlessly before him, the vast number of things he still has to record. In particular, he notes, with an eye on stimulating the sales of future volumes, the Cervantic story of the amours of Uncle Toby and the Widow Wadman. He consoles himself with the thought that his book shall make its way in the world much better than its master has done before it. Paradoxically, incongruously, comically, the recounting of a life in print will make much more stir and a more lasting impression than the living of it.

Volume five begins with a chapter largely devoted to "whiskers," following the pattern of previous divagations on "noses." It is almost as if Tristram, having introduced the subject of death, must for the moment desperately avoid it by trying to return to an earlier mood. The clown must remind us that he is still a clown. He must ring the traditional changes on "placket-holes, and pump-handles—and spigots and faucets." But the letter announcing Bobby's death reappears in chapter two. Walter Shandy rids himself of the affliction of death by exercising his eloquence upon it, as does Corporal Trim, in a rather different fashion, down below in the kitchen. Each of Trim's auditors interprets the death in his or her distinctive way: Susannah, the house maid, thinking how it will benefit her (she will acquire some of Mrs. Shandy's cast-off finery when that lady goes into mourning); the foolish scullion reminding herself that she, in any event, is still alive; Obadiah glumly contemplating the labour on Ox-moor which will now certainly fall upon him since Aunt Dinah's legacy can no longer be spent on Bobby's travels.

Meanwhile, though we are given Susannah's speculations on how Mrs. Shandy will receive the news of her son's death, we never in fact see her reactions. She is left, somewhat cynically by author Tristram, listening outside the door, eventually to become the butt of a joke in ludicrously bad taste. But for Mrs. Shandy, as for Bobby, we feel no grief. The treatment is farcical, though Tristram specifically denies, in chapter fifteen, that the volume is a farce—unless, and this may be an important qualification, "every one's life and opinions are to be looked upon as a farce as well as mine." He immediately launches into a discussion of fiddling, with accompanying onomatopoetic effects, as a means to attack once more the undiscerning critics who think the book a farce. Ironically, this chapter is in Tristram's best farcical style and marks a definite break between discussions of Bobby's death and the next matters of concern: Walter Shandy's *Tristra-paedia* (his system of education for his son), and the final climactic accidental maiming which that son must undergo.

I

The *Tristrapaedia* is to form an "Institute" for the government of Tristram's childhood and adolescence. But in the writing of it, Walter experiences the same difficulties as those encountered by son Tristram in penning his life and opinions: by the time Walter completes one portion of it, Tristram has outgrown that stage so that "every day a page or two became of no consequence." The reason Tristram gives for his father's slow progress (and perhaps his own) is that "the life of a writer . . . was not so much a state of *composition*, as a state of *warfare*" against the suggestions of the devil as to what should go into the book. There is irony here, of course: Tristram's resistance against the devil's suggestions seems constitutionally weak. But then Tristram is a clown, radically maimed in childhood in spite of all his father's efforts to shield him. Most of his wounds, however, are related directly or indirectly to Walter's preoccupation with the problem of evil (as defined by himself: "Prejudice of education, he would say, *is the devil*,—and the multitudes of them which we suck in with our mother's milk—*are the devil and all*" [V, xvi, 375]). Walter Shandy, then, the type of fallen man, is scourged like all those whose pride in human wisdom is intemperate and who "thus outwit ourselves, and eternally forego our purposes in the intemperate act of pursuing them." While

Walter labours over educational theory, young Tristram rudely
learns the dangers of urinating out of upstairs windows, particularly when window sashes are not well hung. Thus the
rite of circumcision, like that of baptism, is administered to
Tristram somewhat inauspiciously.

The conference which ensues at Uncle Toby's house where
Susannah has fled for sanctuary after the accident (to shelter
behind the fortifications erected too late by another maimed
hero) is a comic attempt to fix responsibility for this latest
wound of Tristram's. This is the only one for which Walter
Shandy is not even indirectly to blame (unless he can be held
accountable for the chamber maid's not leaving a chamber
pot under the bed). Corporal Trim, and ultimately Uncle
Toby, are the prime movers in this latest of Tristram's misfortunes. Toby, as commander-in-chief of his garrison, had
expressed a desire for some additional cannons for his forts.
Trim, who is his entire regiment, at once expropriated the
leaden weights and the sash pulleys from the nursery window
in order to construct the field pieces. Susannah's story of the
consequences interrupts Toby's account to Yorick of the Battle
of Steenkirk, and, in particular, the failure of Count Solmes
to follow orders, a failure which led directly to the loss of the
battle. This in turn, according to Trim's reasoning, had led
to his own wound acquired at a subsequent battle made necessary by the loss of the first one. Trim, however, shoulders the
responsibility for Tristram's wound, which came about as a
result of his own prompt obedience of orders. Chains of cause
and effect (and the consequent fixing of responsibility) are
here inextricably tangled.

Tristram, long after the event, completed the *Tristrapaedia*
himself by writing a chapter upon sash-windows and the
forgetfulness of chamber maids—surmising that this is what
his father would have done if time had permitted. He indicates, in his report of the comments which Walter makes to
Yorick at the time of the accident, that the chapter is mainly

taken up with abstruse items of information about the rite
of circumcision. But this trickle of erudition is cut off by
Yorick's reading from Rabelais what he calls the best description he knows of a couple of polemic divines. This turns out
to be the "battle" between Tripet and Gymnast in which the
combatants try to outdo each other in feats of agility, but
never strike a single blow. Toby and Trim are predictably
disgusted, and Yorick agrees with them that "one home thrust
of a bayonet is worth it all." Walter Shandy is, as usual, of
a contrary opinion, but he is not allowed to elaborate on this
point of view. Instead, Yorick draws him out on the subject
of the *Tristrapaedia*. Toby and Trim fail to see the connection; they do not realize that Walter's theories embody as many
mental somersaults and caperings as any parabolized by Rabelais in his fable of Tripet and Gymnast.

The *Tristrapaedia* begins, according to Walter, with a
"prefatory introduction . . . or an introductory preface" on
political or civil government, the foundation of which lay "in
the first conjunction betwixt male and female, for procreation
of the species" (V, xxi, 390). What particularly interests
Walter Shandy is "the foundation of the natural relation
between a father and his child." We are reminded that
Tristram Shandy itself begins with an act of procreation,
followed by a series of attempts on the part of Walter to
exercise his "right and jurisdiction" over his son. The *Tristrapaedia* thus contains in little some of the themes elaborated
on in the book as a whole; in a sense, Tristram's book is his
Tristrapaedia.

Walter's speculations on the "rights" of the father are
interrupted by Yorick's reference to the Catechism, which in
turn leads to Trim's recital of the first five commandments.
To Walter, Trim's automaton-like performance is "the *scaffold
work* of INSTRUCTION, its true point of folly, without the
BUILDING behind it." Ironically, as it proves, Trim grasps the
spirit of the fifth commandment much more surely than does

Walter: he turns "honour" into concrete terms (a daily portion of his pay to help his parents when they grow old). But Walter rushes on to his next chapter which deals with health and its secret: "the due contention for mastery betwixt the radical heat and the radical moisture." This struggle, as Walter describes it, is obviously one between spirit and body (the struggle which might be said to constitute the main "plot" of *Tristram Shandy*). Walter is so little aware of the meaning of his theories that he can propose "that if a child, as he grows up, can be taught to avoid running into fire or water, as either of 'em threaten his destruction,——'twill be all that is needful to be done upon that head." Toby and Trim, in their shrewd simplicity, turn this theoretical struggle, too, into concrete example: the fever they had to fend off during the siege of Limerick when they were camped "in the middle of a devilish, wet, swampy country."

Finally we come to Walter's chapter on the "North-west passage to the intellectual world," his shortcut to learning via a system of auxiliary verbs, which brings us to the end of volume five. Walter demonstrates the efficacy of his method by showing how Trim might discourse on a white bear without ever having seen one—calling to the reader's attention, perhaps, that he himself is frequently engaged in similar exercises in many of his theoretical skirmishes with ideas that for him have no tangible human meaning. Ironically, the system he here recommends to Trim is remarkably like the one he complained about in the Corporal's seemingly mechanical recitation of the commandments. He is proposing that Trim be programmed like a computer and then fed with the proper stimuli to which he will respond, robot-like, in the manner to which he has been conditioned. Body as machine, as so often in comic situations, is here the underlying metaphor. But in the preceding discussion of radical heat and radical moisture it has become clear that Trim can never be conditioned in this way: he lives too much in terms of bodily sensations to submit easily to the dominance of any but fairly elemental ideas. His early training has, in any event, long ago disposed him to react sympathetically to the manifold troubles of his fellow human beings. His artless morality, like that of his master Toby, provides a running commentary on Walter Shandy's unfeeling intellectualism.

II

At the beginning of volume six we are reminded again of the concept of the book as journey, with Tristram as an erratic guide through tortuous terrain. "What a wilderness has it been! and what a mercy that we have not both of us been lost, or devoured by wild beasts in it." The "wild beasts" in this verbal world are necessarily words, words capable of releasing some of the elemental passions which they can also be used to subdue. A good deal of Tristram's clowning with words is analogous to the circus lion tamer's act: the lions roar, but eventually roll over and play dead. For all their potential ferocity, they are absorbed into the context of civilized be-haviour—they become objects of amusement—just as Toby's instruments of war suffer a similar diminution in the "play world" of Sterne's book. The "wild beasts" that Tristram has particularly in mind are the "Jack Ass" critics who have failed to comprehend what his book is about, who have viewed his "travels" from a distance without deigning to join him and to accept his companionship. However, only a page or two later, Tristram reminds us that passion is in effect a wild beast. This is in the scene in which Dr. Slop is annoyed at Susannah's sudden excess of modesty when she is called upon to aid in applying the cataplasm to Tristram's wounded member. In an uproarious slapstick denouement, they end by throwing poor Tristram's poultice at each other. This scene follows hard upon Walter Shandy's learned dissertation on the astonishing feats accomplished by child geniuses, feats which he (in his

Tristrapaedia) attributes to particular modes of education. The poultice-throwing draws forcefully to his attention the necessity for putting young Tristram into the hands of a suitable governor if he is to receive any systematic education whatsoever, and this necessity in turn leads him to discourse on the qualities of the ideal governor. This gives Uncle Toby an opportunity to recommend "poor Le Fever's son" for the position, and Tristram a chance to tell the story of Le Fever which Corporal Trim had been on the point of telling to the assembled servants in the kitchen following his oration on Bobby's death, when Tristram remembered that he had left his mother, as yet unaware of her son's death, listening outside the door to the conversation of Walter and Toby.

With the story of Le Fever we return to a consideration of the fact of death, but in a very different mood to that which prevailed in the account of reactions to Bobby's demise. The story is told as Trim might have related it, though Tristram is the actual narrator (the implication is that he has heard it originally from Trim). The treatment is sentimental. The emphasis is on Toby's and Trim's generosity and goodness of heart, and likewise on similar qualities in the landlord and landlady of the inn where the Le Fevers are staying. The Le Fevers themselves also are imbued with this almost childlike benevolence. Only Mr. Yorick's curate shows up in a rather bad light. The mortal illness of Le Fever is the only event which manages to break through Toby's monomaniacal pre-occupation with the sieges on the bowling green. (Mrs. Wadman breaks through only after the Peace of Utrecht has left Toby and Trim without a war to fight.) Le Fever is a soldier and this in part accounts for Toby's concern for both him and his son. This is the only deathbed scene in Tristram's book, and he pulls out all the stops—eventually a few too many, because, as he rises to a rhetorical climax in his account of Le Fever's fluttering pulse, he, and the reader, suddenly become self-conscious and realize that pathos is as much of a gambit as laughter. Having manœuvred us into being touched by the story of the poor dying soldier, clown Tristram suddenly clanks his bells in our ear, inviting us to step back and admire his handiwork in contriving such a moving scene. This is the sort of Shandean quick-change which has roused readers to question Sterne's "sincerity."[18] But any other manner of concluding the incident would be a breach of the clown's decorum: Tristram may be permitted a tear only if it becomes evident that it is a contrived one and part of his general efforts to "entertain" his audience. The emotions aroused by the death of Le Fever are comparable to those one might feel at the sight of any funeral procession. We are reminded momentarily of our own human frailty, but we quickly shrug off the mood and return impatiently, like Tristram, to our own story.

Before he gets back to his own life, however, Tristram devotes a chapter to Yorick's sermons, the point of departure being the sermon Yorick preached at Le Fever's funeral. He emphasizes the fact that sermons are composed as deliberately as his account of Le Fever's death. Yorick's manuscripts reveal that he often commented on his sermons, very much as a critic might on a work of fiction. (The funeral sermon on poor Le Fever "seems to have been his favourite composition." He had written "Bravo!" at the end of it, later modestly striking out this enthusiastic self-felicitation.) Sometimes on the blank sheets at the end of his sermon Yorick "snatched the occasion of unlacing himself with a few more frolicksome strokes at vice, than the straitness of the pulpit allowed." "These," says Tristram, "though hussar-like, they skirmish lightly and out of all order, are still auxiliaries on the side of virtue," presenting an apparent justification for his own clowning approach to moral problems.

The next problem which Mr. Shandy has to face in con-

18"How much was deliberate calculation and imposture," Thackeray is led to ask, "how much was false sensibility—and how much true feeling?" "Sterne and Goldsmith," in *English Humorists* (Macmillan's Pocket Classics, New York, 1923), p. 225.

nection with his son is the exaggerated nature of the account of his maiming which gossip has made common in the neighbourhood. His solution is to put Tristram into breeches forthwith and thus symbolically proclaim his manhood. The breeching of young Tristram is a matter of serious concern to Walter Shandy and had been discussed by him and Mrs. Shandy (or rather talked about by Walter and acceded to by his wife) in "two several *beds of justice* . . . held for that purpose." He had also, predictably, consulted authority in the person of Albertus Rubenius on the matter, with, as usual, little practical effect. He does, however, order the breeches to be made.

The remainder of volume six is devoted to an account of Uncle Toby's bowling green campaigns and the vulnerable state in which he was left when they were interrupted by the Treaty of Utrecht—so vulnerable that his affections, heretofore fully engaged by his model battles and sieges, became entangled in a conflict of another kind—an amorous one with the Widow Wadman. The "campaigns" are a world that Toby creates for himself as an insulation against the "real" world. In a sense, he is constantly besieged by the importunate demands of life which he fends off in various ways. His carefully constructed replicas of continental battle fields are metaphorical representations of the reality,[19] but reproduced in this fashion they become amusing games rather than occasions for suffering and death. The din of the cannons is replaced by the puffs of smoke from Trim's Turkish pipe; the prefabricated towns are designed for easy demolition and they can be re-assembled on the morrow; there are not even toy soldiers to fall—only Toby as *deus ex machina* and his faithful servant Trim.

[19]Sterne may have modelled his descriptions of Toby's mock battle fields to some extent on the travelling "raree shows" which were a common form of public entertainment in the eighteenth century; see J. M. Stedmond, "Uncle Toby's 'Campaigns' and Raree-Shows," *N & Q*, n.s. III (1956), 28–29.

There is an obvious analogy between this "world" created by Toby, and Tristram Shandy's "world" of words.[20] Tristram, too, fends off the spleen by transforming his trials and tribulations into symbolic form. But his symbols are the all too human counters of language, subject to the frailties of the human condition in a way that Toby's model world is not. Toby takes his "plot," the narrative line of his campaigns, from the course of the war itself. Tristram follows, at a distance, the events of his own life, neutralizing them to some extent (even as Toby, in his different way, renders his battles harmless) by making them the material for comedy. Toby can operate safely within the confines of his bowling green only because of his particular nature: his benevolence, his guilelessness, his belief in a world basically good, ruled over by a kindly deity (as manifested in his various references to God). Tristram however is much more volatile, much more "aware" of life's vicissitudes. The "devil" is more often in his thoughts than God. The tangled skein of his life (represented graphically in the last chapter of volume six) can never be reduced to the simple order of Toby's. He may be maimed, but he is not neutered.

Death for Uncle Toby (despite his previous exposure to it in all its violence on the battle field) is symbolized by the passing of Le Fever, an occasion for pathos, but not for terror; an occasion to reflect, as Yorick does in his funeral sermon, "That so soft and gentle a creature, born to love, to mercy, and kindness, as man is, was not shaped for [war]," at least, not by nature. In his apologetical oration, in which he defends himself against Walter's charge that he is actually sorry to have peace interrupt bloodshed, Toby defines war as "the getting together of quiet and harmless people, with their swords in their hands, to keep the ambitious and turbulent within bounds" (VI, xxxii, 462). But, for Tristram, life itself

[20]See Sigurd Burckhardt, "*Tristram Shandy*'s Law of Gravity," *ELH*, XXVIII (1961), 70–88.

is a war—a comic war, admittedly, a war with words, but words
which are after all man's principal means of coming to terms
with the welter of existence. In volume seven, when for the
first time, apart from the numerous brief authorial digressions
and the slightly longer "Preface," he steps forward full length
in his own person, it is "this son of a whore" Death who drives
him forth on his travels, "the vile cough" which he dreaded
"worse than the devil." Thus the end of a war cost Uncle
Toby his paradise and forced him to eat of the tree of knowledge by exposing him to the guiles of the Widow Wadman.
Tristram flees from Shandy Hall when Death knocks at his
door, flees for his life from England, and tries to lose his
hunter by posting recklessly through France. Here is the
life-as-journey motif unvarnished and undisguised, deliberately
following on the detailed description of the static (though
threatened) world of Uncle Toby.

III

At the beginning of volume seven, Tristram speaks of his
book as a machine. Heretofore, it has been used mainly for
travelling backwards and forwards in time past. Now, with
Death's knock at the door, time future suddenly becomes of
pressing interest, and the book becomes a vehicle for recording
a wild journey through space designed to keep the threat of
the future at bay. The channel crossing provides the first
catharsis—thoughts of Death are partially purged by the non-
fatal malady of sea-sickness. Arrived in France, Tristram re-
treats characteristically behind a bookish façade. He does not
describe the country through which he hastes, but burlesques
the conventional accounts of it contained in travel books. Thus
he places life, and consequently Death, at several removes.
But when, at Boulogne, he allows himself to take note of
une chère fille as she trips by, he is immediately conscious
again of "that death-looking, long-striding scoundrel of a

scare-sinner" who is posting after him. At Montreuil he observes the inn-keeper's daughter, but again rather as a foil to those travel writers who insist on observing famous buildings; however, thoughts of Death interpose themselves once more, and he posts on. The thoughts are not easily shaken, and he speculates on the desirability of keeping his rendezvous with the Disposer in some decent inn, away from the painful solicitations of loved ones. But he at once stipulates that the inn should not be the one at Abbeville where he is at this moment staying. References to Death weave a sober counterpoint through the clownish travelogue: "Death," says Tristram, "might be much nearer me than I imagined"; and on the next page he reveals that "the mode and manner of this great catastrophe . . . takes up and torments . . . [his] thoughts as much as the catastrophe itself."

In talking of the abbey of Saint Austreberte at Montreuil, Tristram ambiguously hints that belief in Christ will not last fifty years more. He reaffirms this opinion a page or two later in his mock discussion of the diminishing stature of human souls, and blesses Jupiter and every other heathen god and goddess who will then come into play again with Priapus at their tails. This passage appears in the chapter following a short mock sermon on the text "Make them like unto a wheel" (Psalms, 83.13) which Tristram takes to be a prophetic judgment on the grand tour as a means of educating children, and which includes an affirmation of the necessity for "getting out of the body, in order to think well," since human reason "is, half of it, SENSE; and the measure of heaven itself is but the measure of our present appetites and concoctions" (VII, xiii, 494).

What Tristram offers us in his account of his travels is neither Reason nor Sense but an erratic series of loosely connected observations, remarks, and bookish references, frequently of a burlesque nature when conventional travel literature is what he has in mind. Tristram (self-described as "a

man with pale face, and clad in black") posts into Paris to
the crack of the postilion's whip. But we are offered no description of the city—only some brief impressions, eccentrically
presented, including data on the nine hundred streets which
the city contained at the survey of 1716. Soon he is led into
an explanation of the dangers for the traveller of allowing
one's spleen to be activated by the trials of the journey (a
matter Yorick is to discuss more fully in *A Sentimental Journey*), and before long he is telling his anecdote about the
abbess of Andoüillets and the novice, Margarita, and their
difficulties with the mules.

As the journey advances, as he passes Paris and penetrates
into the South, references to Death become less frequent. He
is seeking to avoid Death, the unavoidable, or at least to forget
him temporarily. His main concern, though, he has said, is
to learn how to die. This preoccupation with Death may seem
strange in a clown (if one has forgotten for the moment Shakespeare's fools). But Death, in the clown's sense, is life's last
joke. The clown capers, drawing attention to mutability, in
order to render mutability bearable, to make it seem, if not
less lethal, at least less serious. If man can laugh, presumably
so can his Creator, and a god with a sense of humour (who
might be imagined, terrifyingly, laughing *at* man) is, the
clown implies, capable of laughing *with* man, just as the
audience in part identifies with the fool in the very act of
boisterously rejecting his foolishness in a gust of mirth. Tristram makes game of the misfortunes of life; he makes, as he
remarks in connection with the selling of his wrecked chaise
to the pert vamping chaise-undertaker, "a penny of every one
of 'em as they happen." Disasters are grist for his mill, inasmuch as they can be turned into comedy. If life could not be
seen as ludicrous, the clown would lose his reason for being.
Thus Tristram can, reasonably, though comically, castigate
himself for blaming Fortune for pelting him all his life long
with so many small evils. His only cause for anger is that she

has not sent him great ones: "a score of good cursed, bouncing losses, would have been as good as a pension to me." Meanwhile, small frustrations continue to thwart traveller Tristram: the ass with the large panniers on its back that blocks his way at the gate at Lyons; the commissary who demands payment for a trip Tristram has not taken; the lost "remarks" which the chaise-vamper's wife has used for curl-papers; to mention only three "vexations." The volume closes with his leisurely traversing of the plains of Languedoc on the back of a mule, with frequent stops, including one to dance with the "sun-burnt daughter of Labour" and her fellow workers.

IV

The final two volumes of Tristram's book are mainly, though by no means entirely, devoted to the amours of Toby and the Widow Wadman. With head full of recollections of his dance with the country nymphs ("Just disposer of our joys and sorrows, cried I, why could not a man . . . dance, and sing, and say his prayers, and go to heaven with this nut brown maid?"), Tristram finds it even more difficult than usual to settle to the task at hand and develop his narrative in anything remotely like a straight line. He starts a number of hares, following none of them very far: a few brief remarks about his methods of composition; a short passage in the manner of Rabelais; an idiosyncratic chapter on water-drinkers and love, leading up to the revelation that Uncle Toby is *not* a water-drinker: "one would think," says Tristram, "I took pleasure in running into difficulties of this kind, merely to make fresh experiments of getting out of 'em." But by chapter eight he has managed to plunge into his story of Toby's encounter with love. Despite interruptions, this is the most straightforward piece of narrative in the entire book.[21] It

---

[21]Burckhardt, *ibid.*, has suggested that it may well contain in essence the "key" to the rest of the book.

begins with an account of Mrs. Wadman kicking aside the
established nightly ritual of Bridget's pinning, for the sake
of warmth, of the bottom of her mistress's long nightgown—
a rebellion which is occasioned by the arrival of Uncle Toby
from London, and his temporary residence in her house while
his own is being readied for occupancy. "From all of which,"
comments Tristram, "it was plain that widow *Wadman* was
in love with my uncle *Toby*."

Uncle Toby for his part, with his mind full of fortifications, has no notion that Widow Wadman is proceeding to
lay siege to him. Throughout his ensuing campaigns, he is
quite oblivious to the fact that the widow is actually engaged
in a campaign of her own. Toby had developed his intellectual
interest in the science of warfare in order to help heal the
ills of his body, but, by his arrival at Shandy Hall, he had
inadvertently stirred the embers of passion smouldering in
the widow, that "daughter of *Eve*." Her consequent efforts
to stimulate Toby's amorous impulses seem as therapeutically
beneficial for her as is Toby's absorption in his play battles
for him, an absorption which in turn renders him immune,
for the time being, to her skilful attempts to involve him in
a contest of another kind. Once more Tristram is exploiting,
for the entertainment of his readers, the humour of human
cross-purposes. He confesses that he himself shares more than
a little of Mrs. Wadman's nature, that he is a true son of
Adam in his awareness of the delights of the flesh. His imagination is easily heated by thoughts of love.

Most comedies have a modicum of "love interest." Usually
the hero is involved in romantic vicissitudes which lead
eventually to a happy ending. But love plays a rather different
role in the works of Rabelais and of Cervantes (at least as
far as the Don himself is concerned), or for that matter
in Burton's *Anatomy*. These books are anti-romantic in
tone; they tend to emphasize the irrational aspects of passion, the delusions to which lovers are subject. Tristram as

clown-narrator is a version of anti-hero—hardly a suitable central figure for romantic comedy. Emblematic of his exploits in love is his bitter recollection of standing, garters in hand, after having proved a somewhat less than virile partner for his oft-apostrophized Jenny. It seems appropriate, then, that his book's main love story should concern the dubiously wounded Uncle Toby and the single-mindedly erotic Mrs. Wadman. The Widow must wait frustratingly through the years while all of Uncle Toby's interest and energy are expended on his domesticated foreign wars. She can only feign to share his enthusiasm in order to infiltrate through the lines and gain a vantage point at his side in the sentry box, where she can, with an appearance of innocence, press her hand against his as he points out battle locations on his maps—can even, accidentally, make him disturbingly aware of her leg. But these are minor skirmishes. No real confrontation can be managed until some hiatus in the other war.

The Peace of Utrecht has in fact been agreed upon by the time Tristram takes up the story in volume eight, but he does not immediately allow Mrs. Wadman to press her campaign. First Toby and Trim must arrange for the demolition of Dunkirk, and Trim must try to cheer his master with the story of the "King of Bohemia and his seven castles," a story which in its turn never gets told because of the constant intrusions of Uncle Toby, who in this instance plays a part not unlike that of narrator Tristram. So we have the Chinese box effect of the story within the story, the digression within the digression, so characteristic of Tristram's narrative style. In this comic world, stories simply do not get told, though in a sense this is the point of the whole "story": one of the main themes of this "story" is the frustrating impossibility of humans ever getting a story told, of their ever being able to tell "all" about anything. And yet Tristram, as story-teller, has, playing the part of the Fates, "established such a chain of causes and effects" that the amours of Uncle Toby and Widow Wadman are destined to follow the course which they do. Corporal

Trim quotes with approval King William's opinion "that every thing was predestined for us in this world; . . . that 'every ball had its billet'" (VIII, xix, 567). This observation sounds the death knell of the story of the King of Bohemia since it initiates Trim's account of the occasion when he himself fell in love. Now we have, then, a love story within a love story, but a story which is in turn a digression from a digression, and which of course does not get itself told without still more interruptions from Uncle Toby, and from Mrs. Wadman who has been all this time eavesdropping in her arbour. Trim's account of how he fell in love skilfully prepares the way for the Widow Wadman's final assault on the heretofore invulnerable Uncle Toby. The fair Beguine's tender ministrations to the wound upon Trim's knee arouse his passion to the boiling point, in the very way that Mrs. Wadman had been attempting to do with Uncle Toby by placing her hand next to his. But now that his imagination had been sufficiently warmed by the Corporal's story, he was susceptible to more subtly romantic tactics: it is sufficient for the Widow merely to manœuvre him into gazing into her left eye in order to "do his business."

In Tristram's world, however, love is something that Toby can mistake for a saddle sore; it is, in Father Shandy's terms, an ass, a beast concupiscent which must be prevented from kicking. The story of Toby's amours is mainly about his initiation into these animal aspects of romantic passion. No sooner has the Widow succeeded in capturing Toby's heart, than she begins to worry about the seriousness of the wound in his groin. Father Shandy has tamed the beast by dividing it, theoretically, into parts—associated respectively with the brain and the liver—the one, "the golden chain let down from heaven," "excites to the desire of philosophy and truth," the other, "excites to *desire*, simply." For innocent Toby, the beast seems a suitably domestic one, whose admirable function is to "make a man marry, and love his wife, and get a few children." Father Shandy, as usual, sets himself up as the oracle, and duly pens a letter to Toby "upon the nature of women, and of love-making to them," in which he gives advice which he himself obviously honours more in the breach than in the observance. One tenet, however, clearly distinguishes him from his son Tristram: "suffer her not," he says, "to look into *Rabelais,* or *Scarron,* or *Don Quixote* . . . there is no passion so serious, as lust" (VIII, xxxiv, 592). He suggests, instead, that she should be enticed to read over "some devotional tracts"! In short, he counsels Toby to stimulate passion in his lady, but to restrict it severely in himself by such measures as dieting and blood-letting, comical wisdom to direct to the unimpassioned Toby and the lascivious widow. However, it becomes apparent when Tristram takes up the story again at the beginning of volume nine that Walter's situation is the opposite of his brother's: it is he who feels the kicks of the "ass," and Mrs. Shandy the one in whose veins a "temperate current of blood ran orderly . . . in all months of the year."

V

Volume eight ends with Walter questioning his wife's motives in wishing to observe through the keyhole the progress of Uncle Toby's courtship; characteristically, Tristram uses this device to call in question the motives of his readers while at the same time implying that they and Mrs. Shandy would be allowed an unimpeded view in the succeeding instalment. Appropriately, since it is now time to tie up the scattered ends, as much as is possible in a work of this kind, volume nine begins with a fresh dedication to Pitt, now the Earl of Chatham, to whom the opening volumes had been dedicated. As Toby and Trim make their way towards the Widow Wadman's house, the Corporal is given an opportunity to tell of the courtship by his brother Tom of the Jew's widow in Lisbon, a courtship which led to Tom's imprisonment by the Inquisition. Toby's courtship of Mrs. Wadman is of course to result in an inquisition of him by her which will have its own devastating effects. Toby will never be so free again as he was during his happy days of innocence on the bowling green. He will have paid the price for knowledge—a measure of disillusionment.

The book ends as clownishly as it began, with Yorick's ringing description of it as a cock and bull story. Toby's matrimonial ambitions are at an end, his virility as much in question as that of Father Shandy's bull. Father Shandy has proclaimed that "every evil and disorder in the world, from the first fall of *Adam*, down to my uncle *Toby's* (inclusive) was owing one way or other to the same unruly appetite" (IX, xxxii, 644). In the book's final chapter Walter laments that whereas the "act of killing and destroying a man . . . is glorious—and . . . honourable," the "provision for continuing the race of so great, so exalted and godlike a Being . . . couples and equals wise men with fools, and makes us come out of caverns and hiding-places more like satyrs and four-footed beasts than men." Yorick, who at the end of the previous chapter "was just bringing my father's hypothesis to some temper," now rises up "to batter the whole hypothesis to pieces," when Obadiah's entrance with his complaint about the efficacy of the bull provides him with his suitably devastating closing comment.

Human love seen in terms of a cock and a bull is ludicrous: the occasion for mirth or shame, "to be conveyed to a cleanly mind by no language, translation or periphrasis whatever," as Walter Shandy puts it, and as Tristram has amply demonstrated with his linguistic sleight of hand. The vision of man as beast is so exacerbating to Walter because of his overarching hypothesis upon which all his other theories are based: that man is *really*, despite appearances to the contrary, an exalted and godlike being. Something somewhere has gone wrong (presumably at the Fall), but man, by using his godlike reason, *can* set it right, can remove these shameful anomalies that a blundering fate has allowed to demean man's splendour.

Walter has no immediate theories about eliminating the present aboriginal means of procreation, but his thoughts are certainly moving in the direction of a "brave new world." Walter specifically identifies the devil (that is, lust) with women, so presumably the elimination of "every evil and disorder in the world" (Walter's noble aim) would entail the removal of the cause of lust, woman, who plays far too decisive a role in the present faulty arrangement of things. Tristram comments on his father's disposition to crucify truth in defence of an hypothesis. Tristram is fully aware of his own tendency to be "lewd . . . particularly a little before the vernal and autumnal equinoxes," a tendency for which his mother was "at no time, either by nature, by institution, or example" to blame, and a tendency from which he extracts a good deal of pleasure in one way or another. But Tristram sees himself as clown—not god. He sees the "glorious" art of destruction in terms of Toby and his Corporal, who can only seem god-like on the bowling green, and not even there once an armistice has been signed. With Maria of Moulins he notes the resemblance between himself and her goat, but he is conscious of the dissimilarities also: his ungoatlike concern for posterity, for time future and time past, and for time present which "wastes too fast,"—"whilst thou art twisting that lock," he says to Jenny, "see! it grows grey; and every time I kiss thy hand to bid adieu, and every absence which follows it, are preludes to the eternal separation which we are shortly to make" (IX, ix, 611). These are melancholy thoughts for a clown, but they are the basic motivation for his clowning. If he takes seriously Walter's concept of man as potentially god-like, he must either write bitter satire on the gap between the ideal and the actual, or stirring tragedy on the noble drama of man's fall.

Both of these alternatives are possible reactions to the

human condition, but neither is a consistently tenable attitude for most men seeking to retain sanity in the face of the ignoble minutiae of day-to-day existence. The comic view which accepts man's flawed nature as part of his essence, a view which achieves aesthetic distance through laughter, is the one which Tristram adopts.

But the more Tristram seeks to do what he claims he is trying to do—to set down a definitive account of one man's life, presumably in order to get at its essential features, its "truth" (and thus to counter the various false interpretations that have been offered by his critics)—the farther he recedes from his announced goal. He tries to freeze the "past" in the permanent "present" of the printed page, but succeeds only in demonstrating the impossibility of his task. But this very demonstration puts the artist's plight into revealing perspective, and, by analogy, the plight of man. It is man's nature to strive after inaccessible goals, and, in this striving, he is a comic figure: the clown pushing a peanut with his nose across a continent. But without this drive on the one hand, leading to small temporary accomplishments, and the ever receding horizon of attainment on the other, there would be no such thing as human life. Paradoxically, if man were ever able to achieve final answers, he would have moved himself to another plane of existence, he would no longer be "human" in our understanding of the term. This, if you like, is what *Tristram Shandy* is all about; it is the "message" of the Erasmian clown. Man can experience the delights of the human state only by subjecting himself to its limitations. If he rebels disproportionately, he may well lapse into frustrated melancholy; if he submits too readily, he may lose himself in tawdry trivialities. But if he can retain his sense of humour and his urge to make the best possible use of his admittedly limited powers, then he can attain a measure of human happiness.

The Faces of Yorick:
The *Sermons* and
A *Sentimental Journey*

IN HIS STIMULATING remarks on Sterne as humorist, Coleridge
notes that he differs from Rabelais and Cervantes in terms of
the felt *presence* of the man of humour in his works. Whereas
the latter tend to be more objective, to distance themselves,
Sterne projects his humorist into the narrative, and thus in a
sense projects himself. How much of himself he has included
in Tristram and Yorick, and how self-consciously and self-
critically he has done so, has been much debated. The popularity of the notion of personae, of masks which the author
assumes quite deliberately to dramatize aspects of himself, to
play roles which we confuse with the "real" author only at our
peril, has led most recent commentators to stress the necessity
of viewing Tristram and Yorick essentially as characters in
their respective novels rather than as representatives of Sterne
the man.[1] Biographers, of course, have not been willing to

<hr/>

[1]See Rufus Putney, "Laurence Sterne, Apostle of Laughter," *The Age
of Johnson* (New Haven, 1949), pp. 159–70. A relevant discussion of

make such water-tight distinctions. Undoubtedly Tristram and Yorick are emanations of Sterne's personality, but they are also self-consciously played parts. There are obvious similarities between Tristram and Yorick, but there are manifest differences. Neither is in any sense a projection of the "whole man" (if such a thing were possible), as the sermons and the letters, for example, make clear. Both Tristram and Yorick are comic representations of the author as author, that is to say, they are self-conscious and self-critical portrayals.

Hugh Kenner relates Sterne to the group of novelists he calls stoic comedians: Flaubert, Joyce, Beckett.[2] They are stoic in the sense that they recognize and accept the limitations of their art-form, comic in that they satirize, burlesque, make game of these very limitations. They stress "the book as book": a typographical representation of "life" in terms of language frozen into twenty-six alphabetical symbols. They are not story-tellers in any traditional sense; they are manipulators of words and sentences. Sterne obviously is not as conscious as are Flaubert, Joyce, and Beckett of the implications of the typographic era, but like them he bases much of his comedy on a confrontation of the written and spoken word. And like them he writes books about writers writing books— writers conscious of the "rules" of their art and anxious to explore their limits. Thus, Sterne, like these others, operates

---

the problem of "mask" and "author" is provided by Irvin Ehrenpreis in his article on "Personae" in *Restoration and Eighteenth-Century Literature*, ed. Carroll Camden (Chicago, 1963), pp. 25–37. See also Donald J. Greene's comments in "'Dramatic Texture' in Pope," in *From Sensibility to Romanticism: Essays Presented to F. A. Pottle* (New York, 1965), pp. 31–53, and the symposium on "The Concept of the Persona in Satire," in *Satire Newsletter*, III (1966), 89–153.

[2]*Flaubert, Joyce and Beckett: The Stoic Comedians* (Boston, 1962). Marshall McLuhan also mentions this aspect of Sterne in *The Gutenberg Galaxy* (Toronto, 1962), p. 252; and John Fletcher relates Sterne to Beckett in *The Novels of Samuel Beckett* (London, 1964), as does Christopher Ricks in "The Roots of Samuel Beckett," *The Listener*, December 17, 1964, p. 964.

within a closed field: he creates a fictional world according to certain "laws," the "laws" which govern the thoughts of the inventor of this world, the "narrator" who is himself a creation of the author, or who is perhaps an aspect of the author.

In *Tristram Shandy*, then, Sterne posed himself the problem of writing a book such as Tristram would write if a character like Tristram set out to write his "life and opinions." He projects himself into Tristram. However, Tristram is a most self-conscious narrator. Presumably, he is in part conscious of his creator, Laurence Sterne, but this is only another way of saying that, like Sterne, he is supremely conscious of the act of writing itself, of what is involved in trying to transmute the life and opinions of a man into a series of marks on paper. He is conscious of the limits within which he must work: not only the limits imposed by the materials of his chosen art-form, but the limits of what he is trying to represent of the life of a man, inasmuch as he himself is conscious of that life. What he is attempting to record, he realizes, are, basically, his narrator's thoughts about his life, rather than that life itself. The patterns of his book, then, its organizing "laws," will be those of the mind, in so far as he can grasp them. As "stoic comedian," Sterne is thus operating in *Tristram Shandy* within the bounds of several closed systems, notably those of the novel, and those of psychology. As "comedian," however, he toys with those bounds, pushes them to their limits, delighting in the incongruities thus revealed.

But the world of *Tristram Shandy* is in another sense not entirely closed. It intersects, for example, with the *Sermons of Mr. Yorick* and with Yorick's *A Sentimental Journey*. Sermons are composed for oral delivery. The words jotted on the page are meant to be reinforced and modified by the voice, the gesture, the presence of a speaker. The "narrator" is there in person; he has no need to project himself in words on paper as he would in writing a novel. It is not surprising, then, that we learn about "Yorick" mainly by implication in reading his sermons. Yorick is in this instance also operating within certain closed systems: the tradition of the sermon, and the religious beliefs he seeks to expound.

I

At first glance, the *Sermons of Mr. Yorick* seem a far cry from *Tristram Shandy*. Sterne himself was conscious of the possible clash between the two volumes of *Tristram* and the two volumes of *Sermons* which appeared so soon afterwards. In the preface to the latter, he sought to "ease the minds of those who see a jest, and the danger which lurks under it, where no jest was meant." In fact, despite some idiosyncratic elements, the sermons do not give one the impression of Yorick as jester, but rather as Latitudinarian divine, presenting a basically optimistic view of man's nature and the human lot, stressing the benevolent and philanthropic aspects of man's character, and tending to explain all apparent incongruities in terms of the providential design of a beneficent Creator.

As sermons, they are conventional enough, borrowing themes and sometimes actual passages from the sermons of others.[3] What is unconventional about them is their connection with *Tristram Shandy* and *A Sentimental Journey*. They were composed by Sterne in his role as country parson, but, as author, he chose to publish one of them in volume two of *Tristram*, fifteen more shortly afterwards, and a further dozen a few years later while his comic work was still in progress. As a professional writer he was perhaps merely marketing his wares, but as an artist he was providing material which he expected to be read side by side with his other publications. In so far as Yorick may be taken as a "norm" in the comic world of *Tristram Shandy*, his sermons are important elaborations on the point of view which he represents. Composed in the years before *Tristram*, they reveal the themes which

[3]See Hammond, *Laurence Sterne's "Sermons of Mr. Yorick"*.

attracted Sterne (or those he felt would prove attractive to his congregation), they show us the role which he chose to play in the pulpit, the mask he preferred to wear as preacher, the face he chose to present to his public before he had fashioned the guise of Tristram.

Sterne's insertion of a sermon in volume two of *Tristram* is sometimes explained as chiefly an attempt to stimulate a market for the others he had on hand. However, as was noted in a previous chapter, considered in its context, the sermon on a good conscience adds significantly to our understanding of Sterne's comedy. Whatever other reasons he may have had for inserting it, as comic artist he obviously felt the need to place it where he did. Likewise, he was apparently anxious to supplement the first volumes of his comic work with further manifestations of his more serious vein. One can account for this partly in terms of the characteristic desire of the comedian to arouse thoughtful laughter, to dissociate himself offstage from the clownish guise he dons to entertain, to demonstrate that the mirth he arouses has a serious core and can teach as well as amuse. However, if one relates Sterne's work to evolving attitudes to humour and the humorist in eighteenth-century England, one can better appreciate why he felt it necessary to rush his sermons into print so that they would be available to his readers side by side with *Tristram Shandy*.

The fullest account of changing concepts of humour in Sterne's lifetime is given by Stuart Tave in *The Amiable Humorist*.[4] As he makes abundantly clear, the comic writer more and more sought to avoid "ill-natured" satire, the laughing *at* various butts, in favour of "good-natured" laughing *with* his comic creations and thus demonstrating his own compassion and goodwill. The attitudes being reacted against were those implicit in a Hobbesian stress on the constitutional depravity of human nature, leading either to bitter satire or the profane wit associated with the Restoration rakes. Addison

[4](Chicago, 1960).

and Steele, Fielding, Goldsmith, and many others, offered humour of a different kind, based by and large on a different, more optimistic, view of human nature. Sterne's comedy, as we have noted, contains satiric and profane elements, overtones which relate it to Swift's bitter humour and even suggest, at times, the sacrilegious laughter of the libertine wits. Sterne had included such explosive ingredients partially for shock value, but mainly because they formed part of his total comic view. However, since his work was appearing in instalments, his total view could only gradually emerge. Thus he took steps to provide his audience with supplementary evidence that his humour was not, at bottom, heterodox, and that his basic view of human nature was benevolent and compassionate.

Yorick, as we have seen, is presented in *Tristram Shandy* as a Cervantic figure, like Uncle Toby a descendant of Don Quixote. He has his weaknesses—not the innocence of a Toby (or a Parson Adams)—but rather, as Eugenius points out, a blindness to the reaction of fools and knaves to witty castigation, and a tendency to over-rate the powers of ridicule and plain speaking as a means of reforming the vicious. Unlike Uncle Toby, he is neither unable nor unwilling to see the flaws in human nature, but he perhaps over-estimates his ability to amend those flaws. However, like Toby, he is essentially good-hearted and benevolent, normally optimistic in his view of the world, and it is this aspect of his character which is brought out in the sermons.

For example, the seventh sermon in the collection offers a "Vindication of Human Nature," countering a Hobbesian or Mandevillian view that man is "a selfish animal . . . that in fact he lives only to himself."[5] To represent human nature in this way, argues Yorick-Sterne, to emphasize this aspect to

---

[5]Quotations are from *The Sermons of Mr. Yorick,* volumes IX and X in *The Works of Laurence Sterne,* ed. Wilbur L. Cross (The Jenson Society, New York, 1906).

the exclusion of others, only encourages such propensities, and, in any event, is a gross distortion of the actual man who, after all, was made originally in the image of God. He is, of course, a fallen creature, but not by any means as thoroughly depraved as he is pictured by "the satirical pens of so many of the French writers, as well as of our own country, who with more wit than well-meaning have desperately fallen foul upon the whole species, as a set of creatures incapable of either private friendship or public spirit. . . ."

In reality, man's appetites and inclinations render him a social creature, dependent on others not only for many of his satisfactions but also for his very existence. He cannot in fact "live to himself"; he could not survive in a state of pure selfishness. The young man, "just got loose from tutors and governors," seeks society, enters into friendships, some of them doubtless foolish ones, but many of them stemming from disinterested affection for his fellow creatures. He learns caution as he grows older, but also takes on added obligations. Soon he is sacrificing himself to the interests of his family. Most men, in fact, are constantly living for others rather than themselves, are frequently moved by appeals for help from those less fortunate, and often act generously and compassionately. Even the most selfish are so entwined in various social obligations as to make it well nigh impossible for them to live entirely to themselves. The worst of men sometimes pause to consider the consequences of their actions, particularly the possibility that they and the universe were created by a just God who will eventually reward them according to their merits. "As little appearance as there is of religion in the world, there is a great deal of its influence felt in its affairs."

In the sermon immediately following this one, Yorick considers some of the Shandean elements in life: the apparent lack of reason and justice in the world, the apparent governance of time and chance in the affairs of men. Some take this undeniable characteristic of human experience as evidence of the non-existence of a providential God. Obviously, they say, the world is ruled by crass casualty. But Yorick-Sterne proposes an opposite use of this evidence: the fact that things do not infallibly work out as we might expect them to is a demonstration of the existence of a superior intelligent Power which can shape the events of this world. This First Cause of all things is the secret and overruling providence of Almighty God. Happenings which seem to us mere chance are part of a grand design invisible to us, a design which, even so, mysteriously and inexplicably does not invade man's liberty and free will. Again, then, the message is an optimistic one: that all things eventually work together for good, despite appearances to the contrary; that there is a providential plan governing the universe.

Such optimistic views are, however, not always easy to maintain in face of the many tribulations which beset man. In the tenth sermon, Sterne turns to the classic case of Job and his "Account of the Shortness and Troubles of Life." Assuredly, man, like all living creatures, is subject to certain immutable laws—above all, the definite limit of his life-span. And, demonstrably, man's few days are full of troubles: wars and the results of wars, slavery and tyranny of various sorts, and all the many individual disappointments and vexations to which man is subject, whether he is placed high or low in society. But is anything to be gained by thus dwelling on the dark sides of human existence? We must learn, says Yorick-Sterne, to understand our real condition on this earth, to take cognizance of all our defects and infirmities, in order to acquire proper humility and to value the more the prospect of that happier life hereafter for which this vale of tears is but a preparation.

However, will we not be likely to react to our multifarious troubles as did Job's wife, who, in the wake of the succession of disastrous misfortunes which befell her husband, advised him to "Curse God and die"? This is the subject of the final sermon of the first two published volumes. Job's reply was "What!—Shall we receive good at the hand of God, and shall we not receive evil also?" As interpreted by Sterne, Job's contention is that good and evil both emanate from an omnipotent and beneficent creator. When both are put into the scale, good will be seen to outweigh evil. Such men as Job, strong enough to bear misfortunes nobly, have been admired in all societies, pagan or Christian. But such strength and firmness do not come from the mere possession of moral principles. The moral philosopher may seek to teach wisdom, to rationalize troubles away. But he does not teach a man how to bear his troubles. The philosopher is full of good sayings rather than good remedies. His consolations are fine for men at ease; they do little to help the man who is in the midst of suffering.

Yorick-Sterne's main point is "that there are no principles but those of religion to be depended on in cases of real distress"; for the governing principle of religion is the assertion of the existence of a powerful and wise God, who made the world and who continues to govern it. Thus if all is part of a providential plan, our complaints about what seem to be our troubles are obviously short-sighted and stupid; inevitably, all must work itself out for the best in terms of the grand design. In addition, the prospect of a future life, where all will be made clear, renders the small concerns of this one petty and ephemeral.

The Rasselasian theme of man's search for happiness is the subject of the very first sermon in the original two volume collection. The insufficiency of human enjoyments has been lamented by men through the ages, notes the preacher, but despite all the eloquent accounts of "the vanity of human wishes," men still continue to strive for similar objects of desire, continue to pursue constantly elusive phantoms. The conclusion he draws is that human happiness finds its only secure basis in religion, "in the consciousness of virtue—and the sure and certain hopes of a better life." As the wise Solomon advises, "every man who would be happy" should "fear God and keep his commandments."

As in the others, the actual theological content of the sermon is slight. There is no elaboration on exactly what is involved in "fearing God" and "keeping his commandments." Again, the main emphasis is on the finitude of human experience, the built-in limitations in life as we know it, and the consequent necessity of positing a life beyond this one. The approach is pragmatic rather than mystical, calculated to appeal to the common sense of the ordinary man.

Benevolence and compassion are virtues often stressed in these sermons. For instance, the third one in the collection, dealing with the familiar story of the good Samaritan, naturally emphasizes the importance of benevolent philanthropy as a manifestation of Christian virtue. Good works are regarded as almost an absolute good in themselves, without much concern for dogma. Yorick-Sterne asserts that we have an innate tendency to "suffer with the unfortunate," to sympathize with them and feel compassion for them. But he must go on immediately to admit that there are exceptions to this general rule: in this instance, the Priest and the Levite who failed to help the man who had fallen among thieves. He can only conjecture that these two are formed of "impenetrable matter, or wrought up by habitual selfishness to . . . an utter insensibility of what becomes of the fortunes of their fellow-creatures. . . ." That a Priest should have such characteristics might seem surprising, but Sterne admits that such "sordid wretches" do exist who take shelter "behind an appearance of piety." The Levite is even harder of heart, since he crosses over to look at the hapless victim, but yet leaves him to his fate.

Sterne notes the possibility of speculating on what passed in the Levite's mind on this occasion, but prefers to go on to a fuller discussion of the good Samaritan, including an excursion into his thinking processes. This is a primitive exercise in stream-of-consciousness reporting designed to demonstrate that there is in some benevolent natures "a settled principle of humanity and goodness." This does not mean that such men automatically act with compassion, but that they have a tendency to do so. However, Sterne maintains that the seeds of this particular virtue are planted in the hearts of all men and "that a man must do great violence to himself, and suffer many a painful conflict, before he has brought himself to a different disposition." Even the hardest natures feel a secret shame for their acts of inhumanity. In fact, Sterne asserts "that a charitable and benevolent disposition is so principal and ruling a part of a man's character, as to be a considerable test by itself of the whole frame and temper of his mind, with which all other virtues and vices respectively rise and fall." Thus the virtuous man *par excellence* is one who shows concern for his fellows, and most men possess at least the rudiments of such virtue. The human heart, rather than the reason, is thus the prime source of virtuous conduct, conduct which is, according to other sermons, a principal ingredient in human happiness.[6]

These two volumes of sermons, then, tend to stress certain principal themes: the human concern with happiness and its will-o'-the-wisp nature in the context of this world; the necessity for self-scrutiny and the contingent difficulty of examining and judging objectively the motives leading to one's actions; the chastening effect of misfortune as contrasted with the dangerous effects of gaiety; the praise of benevolence and compassion for others as one of the most desirable of human traits. These are also the main themes dealt with in the rest of Sterne's published homilies.

[6]Sterne was not, however, simply "a votary of the heart," as Arthur Cash points out in *Sterne's Comedy of Moral Sentiments*, pp. 104–5. "Only a writer who believed that reason ought to rule the heart could discover Sterne's fundamental comic fact—that the heart can and does trick the head."

II

In a sense, *A Sentimental Journey* provides a critical commentary on the *Sermons*. Both are attributed to Mr. Yorick, but whereas the latter offer a series of set pieces full of general statements on how man should conduct himself, the former confronts the moralizing parson with a number of situations which test these generalizations, reveal the gaps between homily and human conduct, and draw attention to complexities and incongruities largely ignored or glossed over in his pulpit utterances. The form he chooses for these confrontations is the travel book, the account of a visit to the continent with the resulting comparisons between home and abroad. Ostensibly, Yorick is engaged in demonstrating the superiority of the "sentimental" traveller over the "splenetic" one such as Smollett (in his *Travels through France and Italy*) in his ability to appreciate the broadly human qualities underlying even the most apparently alien experiences. But the "sentimental" traveller by no means escapes unscathed, particularly inasmuch as he is a "sentimental" parson and the preacher of sermons.[7] France, in its differences from England, provides a means of seeing parsonical *clichés* in a new light, an opportunity for Yorick to undertake the sort of self-scrutiny recommended in his fourteenth sermon, a chance to examine the "springs and motives" of his actions.

The book begins with a generalization:[8] "——They order, said I, this matter better in France—," which is immediately questioned on empirical grounds by Yorick's "gentleman": "You have been in France?" he asks. This is a sally, obviously,

---

[7]See Gardner D. Stout, Jr., "Yorick's *Sentimental Journey*: A Comic 'Pilgrim's Progress' for the Man of Feeling," *ELH*, XXX (1963), 395–412; Lawrance Thompson, *A Comic Principle in Sterne—Meredith—Joyce* (Oslo, 1954); and Arthur Cash's *Sterne's Comedy of Moral Sentiments* which is sub-titled "The Ethical Dimensions of the *Journey*."

[8]Quotations are from volume V of the *Works*, ed. by Cross, with some minor emendations based on Herbert Read's Scholartis Press edition of *A Sentimental Journey* (London, 1929), the punctuation of which is in close accord with the manuscript of the first volume in the British Museum.

at the human tendency to speak with greatest authority on matters of which we are most ignorant, and very shortly, having arrived on French soil, Yorick is, comically, saying the exact opposite concerning the "ungenerous" provisions of the *Droits d'aubaine*, according to which "the effects of strangers . . . dying in France, are seized." Thus early in the journey does death make its appearance, and with it thoughts of a visit to another unknown country about which Yorick has also been rather dogmatic in some of his previous assertions. "They order these matters better in Heaven" is one of the leading themes in his sermons.

In preparation for his journey abroad Yorick has packed half a dozen shirts and a black pair of silk breeches (which are to reappear in the book's closing incident), but no coat to replace the black clerical one he is wearing. His role is thus to be that of priest, albeit not exactly a conventional wearer of the cloth. However, his first concern on his arrival in France is for material things: a fricassee'd chicken, and the threat to his possessions (including the picture of Eliza he carries round his neck) represented by the king's law. But soon, conscious of the incongruity of his thoughts, he is drinking the king's health and rhetorically kicking his portmanteau aside, lamenting the while that "this world's goods . . . should sharpen our spirits, and make so many kind-hearted brethren of us, fall out so cruelly. . . ." Obviously striking a pose, he continues in this vein, admiringly contemplating the fine feelings of spirituality which benevolent and philanthropic attitudes engender within him. Surely, he feels, he is a living and breathing refutation of atheistical materialism or of notions of man as machine. But he has only just expressed his allegiance to doctrines of universal charity, when he is put to the test by the entrance of a begging Franciscan monk. Here then is a direct confrontation of two of his sermon themes: his devotion to benevolence as a main-spring of piety, and his antagonism to the Roman Church.

Monks in the abstract are sinister figures in the sermons, but, awkwardly, this one encountered in the flesh does not conform to the *cliché*: his "was one of those heads which Guido has often painted—mild, pale—penetrating, free from all commonplace ideas of fat contented ignorance looking downwards upon the earth—it look'd forwards; but look'd, as if it look'd at something beyond this world." Yorick is taken aback at the sight of such a head upon a monk's shoulders. Had it belonged to a Bramin, "upon the plains of Indostan," he admits ruefully, "I had reverenced it." But, for all his protests that he is not a machine, he cannot help reacting automatically to the sight of a monk by determining "not to give him a single sous." He proceeds very cleverly to justify his failure to give alms with a fine legalistic argument concerning the greater claims of the needy and unfortunate, particularly those of his own country (whom he has admittedly left behind for the time being). The debate concludes with a peroration in which he distinguishes between those, presumably like himself, "who wish only to eat the bread of their own labour—and those," like the monk, "who eat the bread of other people's, and have no other plan in Life, but to get through it in sloth and ignorance, *for the Love of God*." The poor Franciscan courteously departs, and Yorick is immediately sorry for "every ungracious syllable" he has spoken. "I have behaved very ill," he admits, and can only offer in somewhat feeble justification that he has "just set out upon my travels; and shall learn better manners as I get along." One thing the reader can watch for, then, is the extent to which Yorick's "manners" improve as his travels progress.

At home, he has not been accustomed to meeting monks on the street. He could denounce them with impunity. But face-to-face confrontation is a different matter. The poor Franciscan is a living embodiment of many of the doctrines which Yorick has upheld on numerous occasions in the pulpit: denial of the flesh, devotion to spiritual matters. His own materialism, his own carnality, are thrown into sharp relief by this unsettling meeting. No wonder he protests so vigorously and is so "discontented with himself." Incongruously, however, he decides that he is now in a properly pugnacious frame of mind to set about bargaining for a chaise to carry him on his journey. As it happens, the master of the hotel has gone to vespers, and Yorick perforce must escape from a further encounter with the monk by climbing into the first chaise which catches his fancy, and setting about the writing of an account of his travels thus far.

He begins, naturally, with the preface, which characteristically is a little essay against travelling. His first concern is with the "boundaries and fences" which Nature has set up "to circumscribe the discontent of man." He stresses the desirability, for the sake of happiness, of staying within the bounds of one's native country, where one understands the language and the customs, and where one can in consequence more easily make oneself understood. On the surface, this is a reaction to the disturbing meeting with the foreign monk, and the difficulty Yorick has had in explaining his attitude satisfactorily. Implicit, however, in this talk of boundaries and fences are the discontents endemic to man's limited condition in general, the constrictions of the human state which Sterne often talks of in the sermons, and which are the basis of much of his comedy.

Yorick goes on to reduce the multiplicity of travellers to a few main categories, in terms of the efficient and final causes of travelling. Most are motivated by pride, curiosity, vanity or spleen unwisely to leave familiar haunts for foreign parts in search of knowledge and self-improvement. He himself is a "sentimental" traveller, and the whole book is offered as a demonstration of what this adjective implies. In practice, of course, the book reveals the inadequacies of all labelling of human beings according to types, for Yorick at various times displays attributes applicable to all the categories, with the notable exception of the "simple" traveller. In the preface, he introduces himself in the role of foreigner abroad, fully convinced of the superiority of his own country over all others, and very sceptical of the value of travel as an enlightening experience. He dramatizes, in the person of his traveller, the ironic fact that most of us in the face of the new and strange, instead of becoming aware of different perspectives and growing in understanding and tolerance, defensively harden our prejudices against the impact of the unsettling, cling the more desperately to the comfortably familiar. This is a theme he has previously treated in his sermon on the prodigal son.[9]

The preface, like so much in Sterne, seems offered half in jest and half in earnest. Typically misplaced, typically incomplete, it serves the purpose of alerting us to the act of writing, to the process of transforming a series of human encounters into words on a page. It also contrasts enlighteningly with what comes before and after, underlining the gap between expository abstractions and concrete instances.

He has declared himself a sentimental traveller, a man of feeling—so feel he must, even to the extent of taking pity on the battered "desobligeant" in the hotel coach-yard in which he had taken refuge to write his preface. He tries to persuade M. Dessein, the hotel-manager, that it would be merciful to rescue the chaise from its present neglected state by selling it to him, presumably at a bargain rate. Prior to writing the preface, he had felt himself, because of his splenetic mood, to be in "an excellent frame of mind for making a bargain." Now, rather incongruously, he is attempting to substitute sentiment for spleen in his commercial approaches. But ironically M. Dessein, the hard-headed businessman, turns the tables on him by showing more interest in him as buyer and human being than in the supposed feelings of the abandoned chaise which would, he contends, "fall to pieces before you

[9]Sermon number five in the second two-volume collection published in 1766; number twenty in the collected edition.

had got half way to Paris." In other words, M. Dessein, thinking he can strike a better bargain for one of the other chaises he has to dispose of, professes more concern for Yorick's welfare than he presumably feels. On the other hand, Yorick, the sentimental clergyman, had no sooner thought of his sympathetic heart than he sought to turn tender feelings to practical use. Yorick, one must remember, however, is not without wit. He is very much aware of hobby-horses, and when he chooses to ride one of his own, we might expect him to do so rather self-consciously.

His first exchange with M. Dessein has made him realize that he is no match for him in business acumen. He eyes him suspiciously and then, once more, has to remind himself that he is again becoming exercised over material things, "a beggarly account of three or four Louis-d'ors, which is the most I can be over-reached in." As clergyman, his thoughts should be elsewhere. But he has just begun to berate himself when, with comic appropriateness, he is brought face-to-face with a comely lady. He can but gallantly offer her his hand. "I write," he notes parenthetically, "not to apologize for the weaknesses of my heart in this tour—but to give an account of them." Like Tristram, Yorick is constantly beset by life's comical absurdities. Not too long before he had been apostrophizing Eliza whose picture he had sworn to carry with him to his grave. But his tender sensibilities are now captivated by the first charmer with whom he comes in contact, and he is soon, while still retaining her hand, devising ways of improving this chance acquaintance. He had previously glimpsed the lady in conversation with the very monk to whom he had refused to give alms, and he is much concerned that the priest might have reported his niggardliness. His attitude towards the lady is, to say the least, ambivalent. Noting an air of sadness about her and conjecturing that she has been recently widowed, he feels, as he says, benevolence for her. But he is obviously bothered by the thought that while he is ready to be generous with his sympathies, which seem to cost him little, he has been far from generous in money matters with the monk. So when the monk appears again at this juncture, and as a gesture of friendliness offers a pinch of snuff, Yorick impulsively makes him a gift of his tortoise shell box to recompense for his previous conduct. Naturally embarrassed, the monk can but offer his own snuff-box in exchange.

Clearly Yorick's gift was motivated by a desire to impress the lady rather than propitiate the monk. But the monk's reciprocal generosity and the genuine selflessness of his conduct rebound upon Yorick, who, in recounting the incident, notes that the horn snuff-box has become a sort of conscience for him, a constant reminder of "the courteous spirit of its owner," now in his grave. (Ironically, the monk seems to occupy in this book a place roughly equivalent to that of Yorick in *Tristram Shandy*. He represents a sort of "norm" by which the conduct of others may be tested. And he, too, is dead and buried before his good qualities can be recorded by the narrator.) The flirtation with the Flemish widow goes on. Clutching the monk's little horn box, Yorick contemplates another generous act: an offer to share his chaise with the lady. However, Avarice, Caution, Cowardice, Discretion all rush in to give him pause, and by the time he is ready to act on his first impulse, the lady has, perhaps conveniently, moved a little distance away. Eventually he is saved from any deeper involvement by the arrival of her brother to accompany her on her journey.

Once more the peripatetic parson's claims to benevolent altruism have been duly tested and implicitly judged. In this series of encounters, neither Yorick nor his sentimental doctrines are obtrusively satirized, but both are placed in an appropriately human context and their necessary limitations sympathetically exposed. Yorick at one point accuses Smelfungus of distorting everything he sees with his own ill nature.

He himself professes to be one "who interests his heart in every thing." In point of fact, as his own claims recognize, his account of his travels is as much a description of an inner as of an outer landscape. His own humanitarianism, he attributes half-playfully to his "having been in love with one princess or another" almost all his life. He is inclined toward mean actions, he says, only when he is between passions. But his generosity, which he can on occasion discuss wittily, is frequently tested as he proceeds on his road. On his departure from Montreuil, he is faced with a group of "the sons and daughters of poverty." There are sixteen in all, but he has predetermined that he will give only eight sous during this, his first public display of his charity in France. By the style of his giving, he seeks to overcome the disparity between their needs and what he has chosen to contribute. He distributes his largesse mainly according to impulse springing from impressions made on him by the various beggars. In his retrospective account, the whole incident sounds like a carefully calculated public performance. Far from showing the impulsive goodness of the feeling heart, it seems too contrived to have much connection with genuine benevolence. Yorick seems much too conscious of the effect he desires to make on his audience. He ignores completely the possibility of turning his professed sympathy for the poor into anything more concrete than this handing out of a few pitifully inadequate coins. And on the basis of this he prides himself on his sensibility! He flirts with the idea of philanthropy in the same way as he flirts with the idea of love in his encounter with the Flemish widow, in neither case allowing his emotions to become more than superficially involved. The whole pose of the man of sensibility seems designed to gain credit for tolerance and sympathy and benevolent good nature, without once allowing the deeper feelings to be moved. The emphasis is on polite manners, suave behaviour. It is part of the human comedy that only thus can the ideal of the urbane "man of feeling" be realized in the face of real human suffering. The sensitive man, confronted with human misery, can retain his equilibrium only by keeping a tight rein on his sympathies.

A sort of knowing mockery has sometimes been claimed to be Sterne's attitude to his sentimental traveller, or at least to the reader who takes him seriously.[10] But Sterne is surely half in love with the character of Yorick. He does not really make game of him; both he and Yorick are part of the larger game called life. When Sterne laughs at Yorick, as he of course often does, he is laughing at an aspect of himself, and at the whole human propensity to play the modish role. The comedy is gentle, there are no guffaws. There is no thought of correcting Yorick, only of portraying him clearly, and thus keeping him (and us) aware of his pretensions by means of shrewd pinpricks whenever he shows signs of floating off in his bubble.

As in *Tristram Shandy*, the basic comic method is the jarring juxtaposition. La Fleur's horse has thrown him as he tries to ride past a dead ass. Yorick curiously observes the oaths with which his valet relieves his feelings, noting that his own nature is too sensitive to allow him such harsh exclamations as "Le Diable!" and "Peste!" He has no thoughts for the dead ass. However, at the very next post-house they come upon the animal's owner, mourning its loss as if it were that of a son. Yorick's comment is "Did we love each other, as this poor soul but loved his ass—'twould be something——." He wants now to meditate gravely on the sad story he has just heard, but his driver "gave an unfeeling lash to each of his beasts and set off clattering like a thousand devils." The whole substance of his meditation is jarred out of him as he calls ineffectually to the driver to reduce his speed. When he is too upset to benefit from it, their pace is slowed by a hill. "Here am I," says Yorick, "sitting as candidly disposed to make the best of the worst, as ever Wight was—and all runs counter." This is

[10]See Ernest Nevin Dilworth, *The Unsentimental Journey of Laurence Sterne* (New York, 1948).

Tristram's plight all over again. Yorick's solution is to fall asleep.

His sensitive heart is next exposed once more in passing to the attractions of Madame de L***, the Flemish widow (a rather less aggressive relict, incidentally, than the one featured in *Tristram Shandy*). She promises, in a letter, to tell him her sad story if he will call upon her in Brussels, and he luxuriates for a time in thoughts of comforting this "fairest of women" by sitting, handkerchief in hand, "in silence the whole night beside her." Soon, however, he is smitten with pangs of guilt at this apparent infidelity to his dear Eliza to whom he has sworn to devote his entire affections. In an ecstasy of remorse, he kneels on the ground, swearing he would not go to Brussels, even if the road there led to heaven, unless Eliza accompanied him. But then comes his ironic acknowledgment of human frailties: "In transports of this kind, the heart in spite of the understanding, will always say too much." And in fact in the very next chapter he is easily inveigled by his romantically inclined servant La Fleur into sending a rather compromising letter to Madame de L***, modelled ironically on one sent by a drummer in La Fleur's former regiment to a corporal's wife.

Not surprisingly, Yorick's first encounter of moment when he reaches Paris is another innocently romantic one, this time with a beautiful glove-seller, from whom he asks directions and whose pulse he cannot resist feeling, with a consequent urge to open his purse to buy a couple of pairs of gloves which he does not really want and which are too large for him. Here then is another wry comment on Yorick's benevolence and generosity and concern for others. The romantic incident ends on a rather mercenary note. Throughout, as usual, Yorick seems to be playing a part. At one point he reflects on how he would have looked to his friend Eugenius if he could have seen him sitting in his black coat "counting the throbs" of the glove-seller's pulse "with as much true devotion as if . . . watching the critical ebb or flow of her fever." One feels it is almost as if Yorick had gone out deliberately in search of just such an experience so that he could include it in his account of his travels.

The next chapter in *A Sentimental Journey* takes him to the Opera Comique, where in rapid succession he meets an old French officer who reminds him of Toby Shandy, shortly finds himself remembering an encounter with the Marquesina de F*** at a concert in Milan, is sentimentally affected by the plight of a dwarf who cannot see the stage because he is behind a large, unyielding German, is suitably shocked when the groundlings, having spied an Abbé seated behind a couple of "grissets," insist that the priest hold up his hands, and ends the first volume of his *Journey* with the anecdote of Madame de Rambouliet (Sterne's spelling) at whose "fountain" he had served with "respectful decorum." This *mélange* of incident and recollection, sentimental and sociological, is designed to demonstrate that, as the old officer puts it "the advantage of travel . . . was by seeing a great deal both of men and manners; it taught us mutual toleration, and . . . mutual love." Yorick's mind apparently flits at random, but the resulting juxtapositions are carefully chosen for their comic incongruities. With the best of intentions, he frequently involves himself in risible situations. He seeks to help a small boy to cross a road, and discovers he has grasped the hand of a forty-year-old dwarf. He tries to be the soul of courtesy to the Marquesina de F*** and to Madame de Rambouliet; in one case he ends up going off with the lady in her carriage, in the other he finds himself assisting her out of her carriage to answer a call of nature. He looks for the "distinguishing marks of national characters" in "nonsensical minutiae," and claims to be little startled by things new and strange. Yet he is unduly disturbed by what seems to him to be a preponderance of dwarfs in Paris, and is obviously upset at the vulgar treatment of the Abbé by the theatre crowd. He claims to pay more attention to the implications of looks and gestures than to actual words, but he must confess that he "blush'd at many a word the first month," even though he maintains he found them "inconsequent and perfectly innocent the second." The comedy is gentle, but everywhere evident. Yorick's human frailties constantly betray him as he strives to live up to his self-imposed ideal. The effect is cumulative. One by one the various incidents define for us the character of the narrator.

Early in volume two he gives a crown and some fatherly advice (he has just been thinking of Polonius) to a young *fille de chambre* whom he encounters in a bookshop. As usual, he is most easily moved to generosity by the sight of a pretty face. But he is no sooner back at his hotel than he finds that he is being inquired after by the police and must face the fact that he is in a country at war with his own, and is without a passport. He may well be clapped into the Bastille. But he manages to convince himself that the terror which the name of the dread prison arouses is in fact more in the word and its associations than in the actual confinement itself, until his comforting meditations are interrupted by the words "I can't get out," repeated over and over by a caged starling. The bird's appeal in English has heretofore won no sympathy from uncomprehending Frenchmen, and its words are, Yorick reports, to have as little effect in England when it is in due course transported there. But for Yorick, the man of sensibility, the encounter with a caged starling, miraculously able to bemoan its fate in human sounds, more effectively stirs his imagination to a full realization of the meaning of Liberty than all the vaguely menacing aura of the Bastille and its minions. Very much as he was wont to do in the sermons, he now conjures up an exemplary instance to represent all the terrors of imprisonment, and he emotionally describes an imaginary poor wretch who has wasted away in a dungeon for thirty years. He bursts into tears at his own eloquence, and then, anticlimactically, directs La Fleur to order his carriage for nine the next morning so that he can go to arrange about a

passport. His concern for Liberty in the abstract boils down to
the protection of his own freedom—a freedom, it soon becomes
clear, never in any real jeopardy. But we are more inclined to
smile at Yorick than to censure him for his very human failings.
Characteristically, he does not even free the starling, but
eventually takes him back to England as a conversation piece,
piling on the irony by adopting him as part of the Yorick coat
of arms.

The affair of the passport makes it necessary for him to
appeal to members of the French nobility, though he says he
hates to go servilely to any man, regardless of rank, to seek
favours. However, he runs over the roles he might play to
impress Le Duc de C*****, discarding them one by one. But
then, while waiting for his audience with Monsieur Le Duc,
he chances upon an impoverished Chevalier de St. Louis
selling *pâtés* in the street, and is duly taken by this gallant
soldier's ability to maintain his dignity despite the low estate
to which he has been reduced. He does not draw the conclusion that he, Yorick, should not feel he has lost face merely
because he must beg a passport from a noble lord, but the
inference is clear. And so is the moral: Yorick reports that the
officer was in due course granted a generous pension as a man
of honour and integrity.

However, rather than petition Monsieur Le Duc directly,
Yorick astutely decides to appeal to the Count de B****, of
whose interest in Shakespeare he has learned. He introduces
himself as Yorick, and the Count, not unexpectedly, takes
him to be the king's jester. Yorick tries to explain that the
English have had no jester at court since the days of Charles
II, "since which time . . . manners have been so gradually refining . . . there is nothing for a jester to make a jest of. . . ."
"Voilà un persiflage!" cries the Count. Earlier in their conversation, Yorick had commented straightfacedly to the reader
that he had something within him which could not "bear the
shock of the least indecent insinuation." So now he complains

with gentle irony that the triumph of obtaining his passport is a little stained by his being described therein as the king's jester. "But," he goes on slyly, "there is nothing unmix'd in this world; and some of the gravest of our divines have carried it so far as to affirm that enjoyment itself was attended even with a sigh——and that the greatest *they knew of* terminated *in a general way*, in little better than a convulsion." At such moments in the *Journey*, we are conscious of the face of Tristram grinning knowingly over Yorick's shoulder.

The very next adventure is with the same pretty *fille de chambre* to whom Yorick had previously given a crown. She is awaiting him at his hotel when he returns, having brought a message from her mistress. And now Yorick must put to the test his assertion to the Count that, as far as Frenchwomen were concerned, the only nakedness he was interested in was that of their hearts, so that "through the different disguises of customs, climates and religion," he could "find out what is good in them" to fashion his own by. Confronted by an actual young woman in his hotel room, he soon finds himself sitting beside her on the foot of the bed, with his hand resting on her lap, and with, as he puts it, the devil in him. He knows this adversary will fly if he resists, but, he explains, "I seldom resist him at all; from a terror, that though I may conquer, I may still get a hurt in the combat—so I give up the triumph for security; and instead of thinking to make him fly, I generally fly myself." And this is what he does now, hurrying with the tempting *fille de chambre* out the door and locking it fast before he dares press a chaste kiss on her cheek. Thus his virtue is saved, but not his reputation, for the hotel manager demands that he give up his room because he has been so indiscreet as to entertain a young female in the evening rather than in the morning. What is even more inexcusable is that she was not there legitimately to sell him laces or ruffles, on which, of course, the manager would have earned a commission.

Yorick solemnly resolves to run no more risks with young women, and to leave Paris possessing, if possible, as much virtue as when he entered it. Unfortunately, interested as he is in acts of charity, his attention is caught by an intrepid beggar who seeks alms only from ladies, and is never refused. What is his secret? By chance Yorick discovers that he reaps his rewards by skilful use of flattery. As a poor clergyman, Yorick stands in relation to the French nobility with whom he is now consorting, very much as this ingenious beggar does to his clientele. So having learned the secret of successful sponging, Yorick cannot resist playing for a time the role of recipient rather than dispenser of favours, commencing with the same Count de B**** with whom he had done so well in the matter of the passport. Soon he is on a merry round of dinners, suppers and concerts, all bought and paid for by a little astute flattery. But eventually, artful manipulation, so pleasurable at first, begins to go against the grain. For the sentimental traveller, the price becomes too high. He abruptly sets out for Italy, once more fleeing from temptation rather than trying to master it.

"Like the Knight of the Woeful Countenance, in quest of melancholy adventures," he seeks out the Maria of Moulines of whom Tristram Shandy had spoken, eager to make up for his Paris peccadilloes by plunging into sentimental sympathy.[11] Thus, in the space of a page or two, he passes from unperverting Madame de V*** by convincing her that she still needed religion in order to defend her charms, to mingling his tears with those of poor Maria, who had been driven mad by thwarted love. He is convinced by this encounter that he indeed has a soul—in other words, he is flattered by it rather

[11]In the sermon on "the house of feasting and the house of mourning" (the second in the first of the two volumes), Sterne says that any social occasion whose object is pleasure, while not inevitably corrupting, tends to make one more susceptible to the demands of the flesh. On the other hand, "the house of mourning" must always make one pause and reflect on the kind of world in which we live and on the nature of our religious beliefs.

than being the flatterer. He fondly thinks of himself as the very type of the good Samaritan, pouring balm on Maria's wounded sensibilities, though in fact he seems to take pleasure in stimulating her tears with his queries. If only, he thinks, she could regain her senses, and if only he was not already committed to dear Eliza, how nice to adopt her as a daughter. He is most conscious of her still evident feminine attractions, the ones which had made Tristram in time past eye her somewhat goatishly. In short, he thoroughly enjoys suffering vicariously with this unfortunate, and bursts into an eloquent panegyric on his "Dear Sensibility" on which he prides himself so much.

Yorick is to get one more supper through flattery before the fragmentary account of his travels breaks off, but this meal, in contrast with Parisian grandeur, is with a peasant family, and the flattery consists only in his condescending to join in their simple repast as if he were an equal. He is of course aware of his superior social station, but derives a good deal of pleasure out of seeming to ignore class differences. Like the scene with Maria, this is a set-piece, deliberately designed to show off Yorick's sympathetic heart, his universal benevolence. In each case the reader is left with the impression that Yorick perhaps plays this part rather too easily, almost glibly. He produces the proper emotion for the occasion almost as smoothly as he provided the appropriately flattering phrase in the Paris salons. One is led to wonder whether the country sentiments are much more deeply felt than the city superficialities. Is Yorick, the self-conscious narrator, also aware of such doubts? He protests possibly a trifle too much, apostrophizes the "poor, patient, quiet, honest people" with a little too much zeal. But then, puckishly, he juxtaposes to his praise of their simple virtues, the bedroom farce with which the book ends.

Throughout his travels Yorick has been ostensibly evading compromising situations with women because of his vows of fidelity to Eliza. In fact, as we have noted, he engages in a series of mild flirtations, skirting the edges of decorum, but always taking flight if emotions seem to be getting out of hand. But now suddenly, quite innocently, he finds himself sharing a bedroom with a Piedmontese lady "with a glow of health in her cheeks," and her "brisk and lively" French maid. In truth, they order things differently on the continent! Yorick accepts the challenge of the occasion. It is, after all, one of those educational experiences which foreign travel provides. He and the lady draw up strict articles of conduct to make their occupancy of adjoining beds as decorous as possible. But their flimsy set of conventions is comically shattered by the sleepless Yorick's ejaculation of "O my God," and the accidental collision of his outflung arm with the young *fille de chambre* who has fearfully interposed herself between him and her mistress. It is at this point that Yorick's account breaks off, leaving the reader to devise the denouement, just as he had been left to imagine how the lady and the clergyman had managed to undress and get to bed in the same room without offense to delicacy.

The ending is characteristically equivocal, as is the character of narrator Yorick throughout the account of his travels. He is not a "clown," but he is a comic figure. His "humour" or ruling passion is his concern with sensibility, with the superiority of the feeling heart over the calculating head. The basic comedy has to do with the clash between his efforts to act with selfless benevolence and ready sympathy, and the various selfish, though typically human, impulses which tend to get in the way. Seen in the context of the sentimental vogue which Sterne helped to stimulate, the incidents in the book have one meaning, but in the context of *Tristram Shandy* and the *Sermons* they have other overtones. Comedy and benevolistic morality exist side by side, but each is muted by the presence of the other and by being filtered through the character of the humanly flawed Yorick. Sterne, like Yorick, had travelled abroad. Sterne like Yorick had a sentimental attachment to Eliza. Sterne like Yorick wore black. Art and life are curiously intermixed in *A Sentimental Journey*. But there is a discernible gap between the Yorick who writes of his travels, the Yorick who preaches, and the one who pens a sentimental journal to Eliza. Traveller Yorick is ironically aware of himself, and, through himself, of the human condition. He is addressing an impersonal public, not an audience of one or a rural congregation, and he adjusts his stance accordingly, adding some touches of motley to his clerical attire, posturing a little, like an actor on stage.

Sterne's Comic View

STERNE'S WRITINGS are shaped by the conventions he uses, but *he* also shapes *them*. What he says is conditioned, and to an extent determined, by the forms of language and the traditions of literary art. But as a creator, as a forger of new patterns, he breaks through the limits which he inherits. He takes as his basic theme the comedy of human efforts at communication, in particular, communication by means of the printed word. To puzzle over what in fact Sterne communicates—what his "message" or his "meaning" is—may be simply to reveal how well he has succeeded in demonstrating the difficulties of communicating.

A Sentimental Journey is a fragment, a series of impressions. It breaks off in mid-sentence. For a good deal of its meaning, it depends on its relationship to *Tristram Shandy*: on the comparison between Tristram and Yorick, and between Tristram's travels recorded in volume seven of his book and Yorick's account of his peregrinations. In the later book Sterne experiments with a more sympathetic narrator, one not so intent on impudently cocking a snook. But the central strategy is similar: each book presents the semi-defensive musings of the narrator on his own and related human failings, and each is designed to arouse the reader's awareness of his own comparable shortcomings. Neither work aims at anything so drastic as reform. As comic explorations of the human psyche, they seek the understanding represented by laughter. Amusement comes from seeing the joke, from getting the point.

Ham-strung by his limitations, man is certainly a ludicrous creature. As portrayed by many twentieth-century writers, his lot is bitterly absurd. But Sterne's comedy is not of the dark "modern" kind. He does mingle pathos with his smiles, but underlying all his humour is a belief in an eventual "happy ending"—as Coleridge put it, finite human experience is measured against the infinite. He states his belief in a beneficent deity in a fairly straightforward manner in the sermons. These contain no evidence of doubt or scepticism. What he is critical of in his comic works is man's failure to grasp the significance of his limitations, to recognize that, granted an optimistic view of the universe, man's terrestrial role is a comic one; that he is a participant in what amounts to a complicated game and, in the end, all his trials and tribulations will be seen as apparent rather than real—all part of an intricate design, all according to the "rules."

Meanwhile, man is fated to struggle on blindly in his limited sphere for his appointed span, quite incapable of threading his way through to the heart of what Alexander Pope calls the "mighty maze." When he acts as if he does understand his destiny and in fact can control it, he is more than usually comical. Human pretensions to wisdom and to knowledge of final truths are a constant source of fun in *Tristram Shandy*. But equally so are human blindnesses to other aspects of man's nature: Toby's naïveté about passions, and, in *A Sentimental Journey*, Yorick's obtuseness about selfish motives. Awareness of the implications of the human condition—this is what Sterne's comic writings seek to stimulate.

Thinking of the sermons, one might say that all his books

deal with the great themes of sin and death, guilt and finitude. But this at once makes them sound far too portentous. In the worlds of Tristram and Yorick, the main sin consists of not realizing how funny one is; and death is the final joke which provides the comic perspective, reducing man's incongruous self-importance to properly ludicrous proportions. Tristram, ironically, at times feels guilt at not being able to get his story told more efficiently; he feels frustration at his failure to communicate clearly. Yorick's guilt stems from his growing awareness of the gap between the role he thinks he wants to play, and the one toward which he naturally gravitates. Tristram is on the whole more successful in accepting himself for what he is. Significantly, he takes himself less seriously than Yorick does, while Yorick, in turn, takes himself far less seriously than does the Sterne of the rather maudlin *Journal to Eliza*.[1]

By means of Tristram and Yorick, Sterne achieves degrees of comic distance from the harsh facts of life. But by removing himself in this way, he also stands a better chance of perceiving some design in the seeming labyrinth of existence, and thus, paradoxically, of coming closer to fundamental truths. To an extent, he seems to have turned to writing humour as an escape, as an antidote to melancholy and ill-health. But also, as artist, he was grappling with his experience, trying to give it aesthetic shape. The pattern which attracted him was one which, on the surface, closely resembled the chaos of undisciplined thought. In contriving comic order in this apparent disorder, he was discovering meaning, of a kind, which seemed to subsume the transitory; he was arriving at designs resistant, up to a point, to the trammels of time.

However, as medium for these patterns, as a means of giving them substance, he must use language, that very

[1]But as W. B. C. Watkins notes concerning the *Journal*: "That 'maudlin sentiment' was addressed by a dying man, deserted by his wife and daughter, to an intimate friend, and, significantly, to a woman; it was certainly never intended for other eyes in the form in which it was written for her"; *Perilous Balance* (Princeton, 1939), p. 107.

humanly imperfect instrument. Understandably, much of his comedy deals with the frustrating difficulties of communication, with man's efforts to use the recalcitrant conventions of vocabulary and syntax both to arrive at truth and to convey it. In the silent world of the printed page man meets still other obstacles. Disembodied, soundless, the language of typography is one further remove from the human, and thus is both help and hindrance. It aids the achievement of aesthetic distance necessary for the artist, but at the price of setting up fresh barriers between him and his raw material and between him and his audience. But the comic artist thrives on obstacles. These are the basis of his art—his primary subject—his constant preoccupation.

In dealing as comic artist with the meaning of life, Sterne was inevitably faced with the enigma of the meaning of one life, that of his comic hero who is also a comic author who shares many of the same frustrations as himself. In their respective books Tristram and Yorick may be thought of as analogues for Sterne, but they are also, and this is an important part of the comic strategy, analogues for the reader. To restate a truism, inasmuch as they are successful artistic creations, they are both individual and representative, concrete and universal. They can then be both surrogates for the author and scapegoats for his audience. By means of them, author and reader can place his own foibles in comic perspective, recognize them, laugh at them, and to that extent be reconciled to them. Unfortunately, the reader who, standing on his dignity, fails to note his resemblance to Tristram or Yorick, is inclined to denounce Sterne's books as tedious and trivial.

Sterne's comic "message" is that man is a being not to be taken too seriously. All that is worst in human history stems from man's tendency to over-value his own importance, to interpret his destiny in terms of gods and angels, heroes and saints. In relation to such paragons, he is a poor creature, but these are not relevant standards against which to measure him.

Seen in his proper context, in his own sphere, he has many good qualities, is in many ways admirable. But in seeking to be more than man, he can become less than human—in trying to be a god, he often acts like a demon.

Laughter is a saving grace, a sort of divine solvent for the removal of dangerous delusions. From a god's-eye view, man *is* comic, as Swift's Lilliputians are comic. In learning to laugh at himself man is, ironically, learning to act like a god in the only way that he can while still retaining his humanity, in all its senses. Sterne as comic artist preaches the doctrines of the religion of laughter by both precept and example. The points he makes are not in basic disagreement with the underlying implications of his more orthodox pulpit pronouncements. But by adopting a comic rhetoric he is able much more effectively to explore and express the significance of his point of view. As jester, he can demonstrate human absurdity and at the same time show the way to come to terms with it. Once he has accepted the *necessary* bounds, the essential "rules" of the human game, man can get a good deal of fun out of playing his part. If he remains aware of his own fallibility, if he constantly keeps his limited activities in true perspective, if he frequently remembers and shares, as much as he can, the amusement of the gods at his antics, he will have achieved a measure of "comic" salvation. This is the message of Yorick and Tristram.

Appendix

STERNE'S NOTORIETY as an arch-plagiarist has snowballed through the years, but, apart from L. V. D. H. Hammond's investigation of the sermons,[1] no systematic attempt seems to have been made to assess either the extent of his borrowings or the use to which he put them. The following is a summary of the incidence of verbatim borrowings in *Tristram Shandy* and *A Sentimental Journey* together with their sources, excluding vague and quite unprovable echoes which have, from time to time, been noted by enthusiasts for whom the name Sterne connoted only plagiarism. Such clearly identified insertions as the Curse of Ernulphus or the burlesque of passages from Locke are also omitted from this summary.[2]

Tristram Shandy

I, xii, 29: a sentence paraphrased (and italicized) from Dr. Thomas Tenison, *Baconiana* (London, 1679), Introduction, p. 16; cf. C. M. Tenison, "Sterne and Plagiarisms," *N & Q*, series 8, VI (1894), 6.

II, i, *passim*: data on Uncle Toby's "campaigns" from N. Tindal, M.A., *The History of England, by Mr. Rapin de Thoyras, Continued from the Revolution to the Accession of King George II* (4 vols., London, 1732–45), III, 293; cf. Theodore Baird, "The Time-Scheme of *Tristram Shandy* and a Source," *PMLA*, LI (1936), 803–20.

iii, 88–89: data from the article on *Fortifications* in Ephraim Chambers, *Cyclopaedia: or, an Universal Dictionary of Arts*

[1]*Laurence Sterne's "Sermons of Mr. Yorick"* (New Haven, 1948).

[2]Some additional well-assimilated echoes from Rabelais and Cervantes have been recently noted by Gardner D. Stout, Jr., in "Some Borrowings in Sterne from Rabelais and Cervantes," *English Language Notes*, III (1965), 111–18. These provide further illustrations of the subtlety of Sterne's allusiveness.

and Sciences (2nd ed., London, 1738), I; cf. Edward Bensley, "A Debt of Sterne's," *TLS*, Nov. 1, 1928, 806.

xii, 111: data from article on *Curtin* in Chambers' *Cyclopaedia*, I; cf. Bensley.

xiv, 116–18: reference to Stephinus' sailing chariot from John Wilkins, *Mathematical Magick* (London, 1708), II, ii; cf. Gwin J. Kolb, "A Note on 'Tristram Shandy': Some New Sources," *N & Q*, CXCVI (1951), 226–27.

xix, 148–49: data from articles on *Soul* and *Sensory* in Chambers' *Cyclopaedia*, II; cf. Bernard L. Greenberg, "Laurence Sterne and Chambers' *Cyclopaedia*," *MLN*, LXIX (1954), 560–62.

152–53: data from article on *Caesarian Section* in Chambers.

III, iv, 160–61: data from article on *Stoics* in Chambers; cf. Bensley.

"The Author's Preface" (III, between chaps. xx and xxi), 200: a sentence (in quotation marks) from Rabelais' *Gargantua and Pantagruel*, trans. Sir Thomas Urquhart and Peter Le Motteux, revised by J. Ozell (London, 1737), III, xvi; cf. Huntington Brown, *Rabelais in English Literature* (Cambridge, Mass., 1933).

xxv, 213: data from article on *Bridge* in Chambers; cf. Bensley.

IV, vii, 277: passage adapted from Sterne's *Sermons*, VI (London, 1769), p. 7; originally from Walter Leightonhouse, *Twelve Sermons, Preached at the Cathedral Church of Lincoln* (London, 1697), pp. 429–30; cf. Hammond, *Sermons*.

vii, 279: another sentence from the same sermon in Sterne's *Sermons*, p. 7.

xvii, 293: a sentence adapted from Sterne's *Sermons*, VII, p. 134.

V, i, 343, 346: four excerpts adapted from Robert Burton, *Anatomy of Melancholy* (6th ed., Oxford, 1651; Everyman's Library edition, 3 vols., London, 1948, I, 23, 24, 130; III, 35–36); cf. John Ferriar, *Illustrations of Sterne* (London, 1798).

ii, 350: another short excerpt from Burton, II, 177, 179–80.

iii, *passim*: eleven miscellaneous passages from the *Anatomy*, II, 178, 180, 181, 182–4; three short passages from Francis Bacon, "Of Death," *The Essayes or Counsels* (Everyman's Library edition, London, 1916, pp. 6–7).

ix, 364: a brief sentence from Burton, III, 52.

x, 365: a phrase from Bacon, p. 7.

xx–xxii, *passim*: assorted data from Tindal, III, 208 ff.

xxviii, 386: a sentence from Burton, III, 22.

xxix, 387–89: a fairly lengthy passage from Rabelais, I, xxv, concerning duel between Gymnast and Tripet; cf. Brown, *Rabelais in English Literature*.

xlii, 403: a passage adapted from Obadiah Walker, *Of Education Especially of Young Gentlemen* (6th ed., London, 1699), p. 111; cf. J. M. Turnbull, "The Prototype of Walter Shandy's *Tristra-paedia*," *Review of English Studies*, II (1926), 212–15.

xliii, 406–407: another passage adapted from Walker, p. 149.

VI, xxiii, xxiv and xxxiv, *passim*: more data from Tindal, IV, 81, 327–28.

xxxvi, 466: another short passage from Burton, III, 11.

VII, xiv, 494, 495: two more brief adaptations from Burton, II, 42; I, 417.

VIII, xix, *passim*: further data from Tindal, III, 240, 654 ff.; IV, 274.

xxvi, 579: a couplet from Burton, III, 186.

xxxi, 583: reference from Burton regarding Hilarion the hermit, III, 191.

xxxiii, 587: ammunition from Burton for Walter Shandy's speech on love, III, 13.

xxxiv, 592: more help from Burton for Walter Shandy's letter to Uncle Toby, III, 193–94.

A Sentimental Journey

Fragment re Abdera: adapted from Burton, III, 109; cf. Ferriar, *Illustrations of Sterne*.

Anecdote re dwarf: sentence adapted from Scarron, *The Whole Comical Works*, trans. by Mr. Tho. Brown, Mr. Savage, and others (London, 1700), I, 235; cf. W. A. Eddy, "Tom Brown and *Tristram Shandy*," *MLN*, XLIV (1929), 379–81.

This summary of the incidence of Sterne's borrowings shows that they are by far most extensive in volume five of *Tristram Shandy*, in both number and length.[3] Among the "sources,"

[3]When viewed in relation to the increase of borrowings in volume V, the following quotation from a letter written by Sterne to his friend John Hall-Stevenson in June, 1761, takes on a new significance: "To-morrow morning, (if Heaven permit) I begin the fifth volume of Shandy–I care

Chambers' *Cyclopaedia* and Tindal's *History* are used, as one would expect from their nature, merely as reference books from which facts concerning fortifications and military campaigns are culled to lend authenticity to the accounts of Uncle Toby's "hobby-horse." Wilkins' *Mathematical Magick* performs a similar function. Walker's treatise on education likewise supplies a few details for Mr. Shandy's *Tristrapaedia* and also furnishes a passage ideal for purposes of burlesque. Ozell's Rabelais, apart from a single sentence (and a few stray words[4]), provides Yorick with his description of the encounter between Gymnast and Tripot in volume five, chapter twenty-nine, and this is plainly stated to be out of "a book from his right-hand coat pocket." Burton, the source most heavily drawn upon, is used mainly as a common-place book of suitable quotations from ancient authors. Mr. Shandy must sprinkle his discourses with learned references to authorities, and Tristram, as his father's son, must also display some touches of quaint erudition. Sterne could scarcely find a better symposium than the *Anatomy* to supply such strokes. The wonder, in retrospect, is that he restrained himself from borrowing far more than he actually did.

Most of the Burtonian echoes occur in volume five, along with excerpts from Tindal, Rabelais, and Walker. The only verbatim debt located in volume one is the passage from Dr. Tenison's introduction to *Baconiana*, and it is printed in italics to indicate its derivative nature. Volumes two and three contain a few background details from Tindal, Chambers, and Wilkins, besides the single sentence from Rabelais in "The Author's Preface." In volume four, three improved fragments from two unpublished sermons (eventually published posthumously) are fitted in. Burton is the only source used verbatim in volumes six, seven, and eight, though Tindal is called on for some historical points. Volume

---

not a curse for the critics—I'll load my vehicle with what goods he sends me, and they may take 'em off my hands, or let them alone—"; *Letters of Laurence Sterne*, ed. L. P. Curtis (Oxford, 1935), p. 140. Another passage from a letter written on July 28 of that year to the same correspondent is also interesting as a possible explanation of the greater literalness of quotations in volume V: "I go on with Tristram—I have bought seven hundred books at a purchase dog cheap—and many good—and I have been a week getting them set up in my best room here—"; *Letters*, p. 142. The fifth and sixth volumes of *Tristram Shandy* did not find so ready a sale as had the first four.
[4]See Brown, *Rabelais in English Literature*.

nine is free of borrowings. In *A Sentimental Journey*, the Lucianic fragment from Burton and the anecdote about the dwarf from Scarron (probably by way of Tom Brown) are the only direct derivatives, and these are so worked up as to be all but unrecognizable.

In the *Art of Sinking in Poetry*, Pope's "Scriblerus" defines imitation as being of "two Sorts; the First is when we force to our own Purposes the Thoughts of others; the Second consists in copying the Imperfections, or Blemishes of celebrated Authors."[5] The definition of the second type is a thrust at the usual advice given in treatises on rhetoric. Obadiah Walker's *Of Education* puts it in this manner: "For *Imitation*; let him *imitate* those he readeth (as is taught in Rhetoric) by *translating, paraphrasing, epitomizing,* and *composing* upon his own subject somewhat like the other."[6] Usually such adjurations were accompanied by a recommendation that a commonplace book be kept. Sterne's borrowings seem to be described better by the first definition fashioned by Martinus Scriblerus, however, and whether or not he kept a commonplace book for this purpose is a moot point. He seems to have preferred to make use of ready-made compilations such as Chambers' *Cyclopaedia*, Walker's *Of Education*, and Tindal's *History*, not to mention Burton's *Anatomy*. He had many eminent forerunners in the practice of borrowing: not only Burton, but Rabelais, too, absorbed much outside material into his *magnum opus*. And, of course, all the humanists, from Budaeus and Erasmus on, were so steeped in the classics that their writings are often almost entirely made up of adapted expressions. While no delver into books on the scale of these giants of scholarship, Sterne shared their enthusiasm for odd and out-of-the-way scraps of knowledge. Like the audience for whom he wrote, he was eager for erudition in a comprehensible form. Like the compilers of Cyclopaedias, he was motivated in part by the effort to achieve some sort of synthesis of the data which experimental science had been accumulating in pursuance of Bacon's inductive method.[7]

---

[5]*Miscellanies*, ed. Pope and Swift, p. 41.

[6]Walker, p. 138.

[7]He was of course not uncritical of such efforts: "Thus—thus [says Tristram Shandy] my fellow labourers and associates in this great harvest of learning, now ripening before our eyes; thus it is, by slow steps of casual increase, that our knowledge, physical, metaphysical, physiological, polemical, nautical, mathematical, aenigmatical, technical, biographical, romantical, chemical, and obstetrical, with fifty other branches of it, (most of

In the matter of borrowing, as in other aspects of his work, Sterne's methods are a strange mixture of the old and the new. He seeks to revivify second-hand material by presenting it in a "singular" manner. Standard neo-classic theories concerning the imitation of models were leavened in the latter half of the eighteenth century by a growing belief that every man had, as Samuel Johnson put it in 1778, "a style peculiar to himself." The concept of the natural diversity of individuals as one of the principal sources of originality was used by many critics as an argument against imitation. Writing in defence of Sterne's style in 1776, Samuel Pratt comments: "Singularity is at all times better than sameness; I mean, it is better to write like an original, than a copier. . . . Every good writer is possest of some marks of excellence peculiar to himself."[8] Judged by such standards of his own time, Sterne might be said to be truly "original," regardless of how much of other men's books he appropriated, since he encased his borrowings in his own very individual and apparently spontaneous manner of expression.

'em ending, as these do, in *ical*) have, for these two last centuries and more, gradually been creeping upwards towards that 'Αχμὴ of their perfections, from which, if we may form a conjecture from the advances of these last seven years we cannot possibly be far off" (I, xxi, 64).

[8]*Observations on the Night Thoughts of Dr. Young* (London, 1776), pp. 73–74; quoted by Elizabeth L. Mann, "The Problem of Originality in English Literary Criticism, 1750–1800."

Index

ADDISON, JOSEPH, 32, 136
Alazon: Walter Shandy and Uncle Toby as, 7
Anatomy: as form of prose fiction, 12, 13
Anti-Ciceronian style: characteristics of, 33–37
Arbuthnot, John, 49n
Aristotle, 51, 66

BACON, FRANCIS, 33, 36, 167, 170; *Advancement of Learning*, 35n
Baird, Theodore, 22n, 166
Barber, C. L., 6n
Barish, Jonas A., 33n
Beckett, Samuel, 5, 133
Bensley, Edward, 167
Bergson, Henri, 29
Blake William: *An Island in the Moon*, 101n
Booth, Wayne C., 4n, 11n, 64n
Brown, Huntington, 38n, 167, 168, 169n
Brown, John: *An Estimate of the Manners and Principles of the Times*, 57n
Brown, Tom, 168, 170
Browne, Sir Thomas, 12, 36; *Religio Medici*, 34n, 35n; *Vulgar Errors*, 16
Budaeus, 170
Bunyan, John, 69
Burckhardt, Sigurd, 120n, 124n
Burke, Edmund, 32
Burton, Robert: and Sterne, 5, 12, 20, 25, 26, 40n, 109; and Hafen Slawkenbergius, 102n
  Anatomy of Melancholy: borrowings from in *Tristram Shandy*,

167–70 *passim*; role of love in, 125; structure of, 15–16; style of, 33, 34n
Butler, Samuel: *Erewhon*, 12
Butler, Samuel: *Hudibras*, 12n

CASH, ARTHUR H., 6n, 24n, 85n, 142n, 143n
Cervantes Saavedra, Miguel de, 96; and Sterne, 5, 9, 12n, 37, 41, 46, 75, 76, 103, 111, 132
  Don Quixote, 128; style of compared with *Tristram Shandy*, 42–43; role of love in, 125
  Don Quixote: as controlling "norm" in *Tristram Shandy*, 69–70; and Sancho Panza, 91; and Uncle Toby, 76, 82; compared with Yorick and Toby, 137
Chambers, Ephraim: *Cyclopaedia*, 166, 167, 169, 170
Cline, James M., 16n
Coleridge, Samuel Taylor, 25n, 162; on Sterne as humorist, 132
Comedy: and satire, distinctions between, 66
Congreve, William, 48
Conventions: comic uses of, 4; manipulation of in art, 10
Cook, Albert, 67n
Croll, Morris W., 33, 34, 35n, 36
Cross, Wilbur L., 143n
Curtis, L. P., 169n

DAVIE, DONALD, 32n
Defoe, Daniel, 18, 28
De Quincey, Thomas, 13
Descartes, René, 52, 53n, 88

Diderot, Denis, 21n
Dilworth, Ernest Nevin, 151n
Dobrée, Bonamy, 30n; on Sterne's style, 32
Donne, John, 35n
Durrell, Lawrence, 5n
Dyson, A. E., 65n

EDDY, W. A., 168
Ehrenpreis, Irvin, 133n
Eiron: Tristram as, 7
Eliot, T. S., 22; *Waste Land*, 21
Elliott, George P., 5n
Elloway, D. R., 24n
Erasmus, 12, 170; *Colloquia Familiaria*, 102n; *Praise of Folly*, 16, 91; Folly, 10; Erasmian clown, Tristram as, 131

FARRELL, WILLIAM J., 42n
Ferriar, John, 167, 168
Fielding, Henry: and Sterne, 4, 11, 12n, 20, 23n, 28, 103; style of, 32; Parson Adams compared to Toby and Yorick, 137
Flaubert, Gustave, 133
Fletcher, John, 133n
Fluchère, Henri, 11n
Frank, Joseph: concept of spatial form in literature, 21–22
Freud, Sigmund, 20, 29, 87; Sterne's differences from, 7n
Friedman, Melvin, 37n
Frye, Northrop, 12, 100; *Anatomy of Criticism*, 7; four forms of prose fiction, 11n, 12

GARRICK, DAVID, 45, 46
Gay, John, 49n
Genre: studies of, 20
Gibbon, Edward, 32
Goethe, Johann Wolfgang von, 25n
Goldsmith, Oliver, 48, 137
Green, Henry, 5n
Greenberg, Bernard L., 167
Greene, Donald J., 133n
Grub Street, 64

HALL-STEVENSON, JOHN, 94, 168n

Hammond, L. V. D. H., 33n, 135n, 166, 167
Harley, Robert, Earl of Oxford, 49n
Harper, Kenneth E., 23n
Hartley, Lodwick, 3n
Hazlitt, William, 31
History of a Good Warm Watch-Coat, 33n
Hnatko, Eugene, 37n, 41n
Hobbes, Thomas, 136, 137
Hogarth, William, 79
Hooker, Edward N., 48n
Houghton, Walter E.: the English virtuoso movement, 26–27
Howes, Alan B., 3n
Huizanga, J., 100n
Hume, David, 54n; on personal identity, 24
Huxley, Aldous: *Brave New World*, 12

JEFFERSON, D. W., 11n, 12
Johnson, Maurice, 68n
Johnson, Ralph, 40n
Johnson, Samuel, 32, 171; *Rasselas*, theme of, 140
Jonson, Ben, 75
Journal to Eliza, 160, 163
Joyce, James: and Sterne, 5, 21, 22, 27, 28, 29, 133
Jung, Carl, 29; and concepts of artistic unity, 20–21

KAISER, WALTER, 92, 103n
Karl, Frederick R., 5n
Kenner, Hugh, 21n, 133
Kerby-Miller, Charles, 50n
Kermode, Frank, 5n
Kolb, Gwin J., 167

LA MOTHE LE VAYER, FRANÇOIS DE, 35n
Landa, Louis, A., 68n
Leda, 7, 8
Lehman, B. H., 28
Leightonhouse, Walter, 167
Le Motteux, Peter, 167
Lessing, G. E., 25n; *Laokoon*, 21
Locke, John, 166; and association of ideas, 7; burlesque of in *Tristram*

Shandy, 51, 79, 95–96, 97–98; breakdown of his solutions, 54; his concept of personal identity, 23–24; his concept of mind, 63; and instability of language, 57; his influence on Sterne's moral philosophy, 85n; psychology of, 28, 29; his theories of perception, 76
Lockridge, Ernest H., 73n
Lucian, 96, 170
Lussky, A. E., 25n

MCKILLOP, A. D., 11n
MacLean, Kenneth, 24n
McLuhan, Marshall, 133n
MacNally, Leonard: *Tristram Shandy, a sentimental Shandean bagatelle*, 45n
Mandel, Oscar, 69n
Mandeville, Bernard, 137
Mann, Elizabeth L., 31n, 171
Mann, Thomas, 5, 21, 27, 28
Mendilow, A. A., 21n, 23
Menippean satire, 11, 12
Meyerhoff, Hans, 23n, 24n
Montaigne, Michel de, 35n

NABOKOV, VLADIMIR, 5n
Nevo, Ruth, 67n, 79n
Newton, Sir Isaac, 9, 53n

ONG, WALTER J., 34n, 63n
Ozell, John, 38, 167, 169

PARNELL, THOMAS, 49n
Pascal, Blaise: *Pensées*, 35n
Peacham, Henry: *Garden of Eloquence*, 42
Peacock, Thomas Love, 12
Pharmakos: Tristram and Uncle Toby as, 7
Pinger, W. R. R., 25n
Piper, William Bowman, 12n
Pitt, William, Earl of Chatham: dedication to, 10, 54; second dedication to, 128
Pope, Alexander, 162; and Sterne, 12n, 48, 49, 54
    Art of Sinking in Poetry: on abuse of speech and the prurient

style, 40; definition by "Scriblerus" of imitation, 170
Dunciad: and *Tristram Shandy*, 53, 58, 64
Pound, Ezra, 22; *Cantos*, 13; poetic theories of, 21
Pratt, Samuel, 171
Proust, Marcel, 22, 28, 29
Putney, Rufus, 132n

QUINTANA, RICARDO, 17n

RABELAIS, FRANÇOIS, 96, 124, 128; as borrower, 170; as humorist, compared with Sterne, 132; style compared with Sterne's, 42, 46
    Gargantua and Pantagruel: borrowings from in *Tristram Shandy*, 19, 167, 168, 169; compared with *Tristram Shandy*, 5, 12, 18, 20, 25, 26, 41, 44; fable of Tripet and Gymnast in *Tristram Shandy*, 114; narrative structure of, 13–15; Panurge, 103; Panurge and Pantagruel, 91; references to in *Tristram Shandy*, 102n; role of love in, 125; style of, 37–38
Ramus, 63n
Read, Sir Herbert, 39n, 143n
Richardson, Samuel, 4, 20, 23n, 28, 32, 106
Ricks, Christopher, 133n
Rosenheim, Edward W., Jr., 6n
Ryle, Gilbert, 63n

SATIRE: changes in during eighteenth century, 48–49; and comedy, distinctions between, 66
Satire Newsletter, 133n
Scarron, Paul, 128, 168, 170
Scriblerus, Martinus, 170; *Memoirs of*, 26, 49–54 *passim*; and Cornelius, 27; definition of "Prurient Style," 40n; Scriblerians, 12
Sentimental Journey, A, 5, 36, 39n, 43n, 44, 48, 67, 109, 123, 134, 135, 170; Yorick in, 46; Yorick's

role in compared to *Sermons*, 143–60; opening of, 143–44; Eliza in, 144, 148, 152, 158; the Franciscan monk in, 144–46, 149; preface to, 146–47; the "desobligeant" in, 147–48; the Flemish widow in, 148–49, 152; Yorick's philanthropy at Montreuil in, 150; Sterne's attitude to Yorick in, 151; comic juxtapositions in, 151; the glove-seller in, 152–53; Eugenius in, 152; the Opera Comique in, 153–54; Uncle Toby in, 153; the *fille de chambre* in, 154, 156; the passport in, 154–56; the caged starling in, 154–55; Maria in, 157–58; Yorick's use of flattery in, 157, 158; the Piedmontese lady in, 159; Yorick as comic figure in, 159–60, 162; compared with *Tristram Shandy*, 161–62, 163

Sermons of Mr. Yorick, 5, 90, 91, 134, 167; Yorick in, 134–35; compared with *Tristram Shandy*, 135–36; analysis of, 137–42; Job in, 139–40; Good Samaritan in, 141–42

Shakespeare, William, 12n, 69, 70, 155

Shakespearean Fool, 9

Shklovsky, Victor, 23n

Smart, Christopher: *Jubilate Agno*, 101n

Smollett, Tobias, 4, 20, 32, 38n; in *Sentimental Journey*, 143

Spitzer, Leo, 42

Stedmond, J. M., 119n

Steele, Richard, 137

Sterne, Laurence: as innovator, 3–4; his interest in time, 23–25 *passim*; his use of stream-of-consciousness, 24–25; his creation of an identity in *Tristram Shandy*, 25–26; his "modernity," 29; attitudes towards his prose style, 31–33; his awareness of mortality, 108–09; his masks, 132–33; as "stoic comedian," 133–34; his relation to changing concepts of humour,

136–37; his attitude to Yorick in *Sentimental Journey*, 151; his comedy of human efforts at communication, 161; his comedy not absurd, 162; as artist, 163–64; his comic "message," 164–65; his borrowings in *Sentimental Journey*, 168; his borrowings in *Tristram Shandy*, 166–68; *Letters* of, 168n

Stevenson, Lionel, 5n

Stout, Gardner D., Jr., 143n, 166n

Stream-of-consciousness, 28–29; use of by Sterne, 24–25; of Good Samaritan, 141–42

Style: in prose works of the imagination, 30–31

Sutherland, James, 32n

Swift, Jonathan, 40n; and Sterne, 12, 18, 20, 26, 48, 49, 58, 73, 137, 165; on satire, 89; style of, 32; *Battle of the Books*, 16; *Gulliver's Travels*, 12, 54; *A Modest Proposal*, 54; *A Tale of a Tub*, 16–17, 26, 48, 53, 64, 97

TAVE, STUART, 136

Tenison, C. M., 166

Tenison, Dr. Thomas, 166, 169

Thackeray, W. M., 118n

Thompson, Lawrance, 143n

Tieck, Johann Ludwig, 25n

Tillotson, Archbishop John, 33n

Tindal, N., 166, 168, 169, 170

Towers, A. R., 6

Traill, H. D., 31

Traugott, John, 11n, 12, 23n, 24n, 53n, 54n, 91n, 98n

Tristram Shandy: and its tradition, 4–5, 11–29 *passim*; its allusiveness, 4–5; as "punitive satire," 6; as saturnalia, 6; as sexual comedy, 6–7; unconventionality as convention in, 7; opening scene, use of comic conventions in, 7–9; opening scene, bawdiness of, 8; opening scene, implications of, 9; order in disorder in, 9–10; narrative point of view in, 17–18; and the modern novel, 20–29 *passim*; "spatial form" in, 22; anti-Ciceronian elements in style of, 34–37; Rabelaisian elements in style of, 38–42, 46; Cervantean elements in style of, 42–46; puns and double meanings in, 44–45; use of posture and gesture in, 45–46; compared with *Memoirs of Martinus Scriblerus*, 49–54; war between humanist and pedant in, 53–54; attacks on abuses in learning in, 58–62; strange working of cause and effect in, 61–62; compared with *Dunciad*, 64–65; implied "norms" in, 67–68; comic tone at beginning of, 68–69; Don Quixote as "norm" in, 69–70; as absurd, 73; as comic rather than satiric, 71, 73, 89; Tristram's digressions in, 74–75; man as mechanism in, 74, 115–16; comic use of *non sequitur* in, 75; characterization by hobby-horse in, 75–76; transition between volumes in, 89–90; Erasmian irony in, 92; and tradition of "wise fool," 91–93; "truth" as ostensible subject of, 95–96; as comic game, 100n; defences against thoughts of death in, 109–11; compared with *Sentimental Journey*, 161–62

other components of: Abbess of Andoüillets, 55, 123; "Author's Preface," 50, 96–99, 169; the canonical dinner, 107–08; Curse of Ernulphus, 19, 57, 93–94, 98, 101, 166; "King of Bohemia and his seven castles," 126–27; Le Fever, story of, 117–18; *Mémoire présenté à Messieurs les Docteurs de Sorbonne*, 19, 72, 73; Mrs. Shandy's marriage settlement, 70–71; Sermon on good conscience, 84–87; 136; "Slawkenbergius's Tale," 19, 51, 52, 58, 103–05; *Tristrapaedia*, 19, 49, 112, 113, 114–16 *passim*, 117, 169

Tristram in: as *pharmakos*, 7; as *eiron*, 7; as "editor," 18–20; as virtuoso, 27; as *rhetor*, 54–57, 62–64; as comic hero, 67–68; as "wise clown," 68–69; his techniques as narrator, 72–75, 88–89, 94–95, 99–101, 102–03, 117–18, 124; his digressions, 74–75; his bawdiness, 78–79, 102; his awareness of time, 79; as stage-manager, 80–81; his relationship with reader, 89; and the reviewers, 91; his Slawkenbergian mask, 104–05; as comic portrait of artist, 109–10; circumcision of, 113; his verbal play, 116; his verbal world compared with Uncle Toby's bowling green "world," 120; his "travels," 121–24; his awareness of death, 121–22, 123; as anti-hero, 125–26; as clown-author in closing volumes, 130–31; as self-conscious narrator, 134–35; compared with Yorick in *Sentimental Journey*, 163

other characters in: Bobby Shandy, 110, 111, 112, 117; Bridget, 101, 125; Aunt Dinah, 61, 74, 110, 111; Eugenius, 70, 108, 137; Mrs. Shandy, 8, 9, 39, 61, 73, 78, 81, 85, 111, 117, 119, 128; Obadiah, 78, 79, 80, 93, 111, 129; Phutatorius, 45, 55n, 107, 108; Dr. Slop, 41, 44, 52, 57, 59, 62, 78, 79–81 *passim*, 83–86 *passim*, 90–95 *passim*, 101, 116; Susannah, 111, 113, 116; Uncle Toby, 7, 22, 41, 44, 45, 50–53 *passim*, 59–60, 64, 73, 74, 76–84 *passim*, 86, 90, 92–96 *passim*, 99, 100n, 101, 103, 105, 111, 113–17 *passim*, 119–21, 124, 125–28, 129, 137, 162, 168, 169; Corporal Trim,

39, 41n, 44, 45, 64, 77, 83–84, 86, 99, 101, 105, 111, 113, 114, 115, 117, 119, 126–27, 128; Walter Shandy, 7, 8, 27, 36, 40, 41, 43, 44, 49–53 *passim*, 58–59, 60–61, 71–73 *passim*, 78–88 *passim*, 90–92 *passim*, 94–96 *passim*, 98–103 *passim*, 105–107 *passim*, 110–20 *passim*, 127–30 *passim*, 168, 169; Widow Wadman, 22, 44, 45n, 60, 64, 77, 78, 81, 89, 100n, 111, 117, 119, 121, 124, 125–28 *passim*; Yorick, 9–10, 25, 34, 37, 44, 50, 56, 69–70, 80, 84, 85, 87, 97, 98, 105, 107, 108, 113, 114, 118, 129, 135–36, 137–42, 169
Turnbull, J. M., 168
Tuveson, Ernest, 24n, 63n

ULLMAN, STEPHEN, 30n
Urquhart, Sir Thomas, 38

VIRTUOSO: discussion of, 26–27
Voltaire: *Candide*, 12

WALKER, OBADIAH, 40n, 168, 169, 170
Wallace, Thomas, 31
Watkins, W. B. C., 163
Watson, Wilfred, 53n
Watt, Ian, 11n, 17n, 23n
Wilkins, John, 167, 169
Willey, Basil, 48n
Williams, Aubrey, 58
Williamson, George, 33n, 36n
Woolf, Virginia, 5; on Sterne's style, 31–32
Work, James A., 17n, 49n